The Samuel & Althea Stroum Lectures

IN JEWISH STUDIES

The Samuel & Althea Stroum Lectures

IN JEWISH STUDIES

The Yiddish Art Song
performed by Leon Lishner, basso,
and Lazar Weiner, piano
(stereophonic record album)

The Holocaust in Historical Perspective
Yehuda Bauer

Zakhor: Jewish History and Jewish Memory
Yosef Hayim Yerushalmi

Jewish Mysticism and Jewish Ethics
Joseph Dan

The Invention of Hebrew Prose:
Modern Fiction and the Language of Realism
Robert Alter

Recent Archaeological Discoveries and Biblical Research
William G. Dever

Jewish Identity in the Modern World
Michael Meyer

I. L. Peretz and the Making of
Modern Jewish Culture
Ruth R. Wisse

I. L. Peretz
and the
Making
of Modern
Jewish
Culture

❧

RUTH R. WISSE

UNIVERSITY OF WASHINGTON PRESS

Seattle & London

Library of Congress Cataloging-in-Publication Data

Wisse, Ruth R.
  I. L. Peretz and the making of modern Jewish culture / Ruth
R. Wisse.
    p.   cm.—(The Samuel and Althea Stroum lectures in Jewish
studies)
    Includes bibliographical references and index.
    ISBN 978-0-295-99479-6 (alk. paper)
    1. Peretz, Isaac Leib, 1851 or 2-1915—Religion.   2. Peretz,
Isaac Leib, 1851 or 2-1915—Political and social
views.   I. Title.   II. Title: Making of modern Jewish
culture.   III. Series.
PJ5129.P4Z97   1991
839'.098309—dc20   90-19350
                                                         CIP

The paper used in this publication meets the minimum
requirements of
American National Standard for Information Sciences—
Permanence of Paper
for Printed Library Materials, ANSI Z39.48-1984

The Samuel & Althea Stroum Lectures

IN JEWISH STUDIES

Samuel Stroum, businessman, community leader, and philanthropist, by a major gift to the Jewish Federation of Greater Seattle, established the Samuel and Althea Stroum Philanthropic Fund.

In recognition of Mr. and Mrs. Stroum's deep interest in Jewish history and culture, the Board of Directors of the Jewish Federation of Seattle, in cooperation with the Jewish Studies Program of the Henry M. Jackson School of International Studies at the University of Washington, established an annual lectureship at the University of Washington known as the Samuel and Althea Stroum Lectureship in Jewish Studies. This lectureship makes it possible to bring to the area outstanding scholars and interpreters of Jewish thought, thus promoting a deeper understanding of Jewish history, religion, and culture. Such understanding can lead to an enhanced appreciation of the Jewish contributions to the historical and cultural traditions that have shaped the American nation.

The terms of the gift also provide for the publication from time to time of the lectures or other appropriate materials resulting from or related to the lectures.

To my husband Len Wisse

Contents

Acknowledgments

T HIS STUDY is based on the series of Stroum lectures I delivered in 1988 at the University of Washington in Seattle. I am very grateful to all those who made the experience so pleasurable, particularly the chairman of the Jewish Studies program Hillel Kieval, its coordinator Dorothy Becker, and Mr. and Mrs. Samuel Stroum, generous benefactors and wonderful hosts. Thanks to the patience and encouragement of Naomi Pascal, editor-in-chief of the University of Washington Press, I managed the transition from lectures to book.

Most of the research for this book was done at the National and Hebrew University Library and Archives in Jerusalem, the YIVO Institute for Jewish Research in New York, Widener Library of Harvard in Cambridge, McGill University's MacLennan Library, and the Jewish Public Library of Montreal. I am ever thankful to the staffs of those institutions for the courtesy they continue to show me through the years. I wrote this book at the same time that I was editing volume 2 of the Library of Yiddish Classics, *The I. L. Peretz Reader;* and many of the works mentioned here can be found in that anthology, enabling readers to set their own impressions against mine.

My brother David Roskies, most generous colleague and friend, was especially helpful in the preparation of this manuscript, though he cannot be held responsible for its flaws. Michael C. Steinlauf shared with me material he had collected from the daily Yiddish press in Poland that would otherwise have remained inaccessible to me. Magda Opalski's friendship and intellectual curiosity make me wish this study of Peretz were more thorough and complete. I am grateful to my erudite colleagues at McGill University, among them some of my closest friends, who have contributed to this work in one way or another. The bibliographical index to Yiddish periodicals prepared under the guidance of Khone Shmeruk and Chava Turniansky of the Hebrew University in Jerusalem was a most welcome, valuable asset. To Khone Shmeruk the field of Yiddish studies owes a special thanks for opening the doors of scholarship and of his home.

In dedicating this book to my husband I am mindful of our good fortune in sharing a culture as well as love. He embodies the ideals of dignity and compassion that we absorbed from Peretz in our youth, along with a sense of humor that makes goodness friendlier.

Introduction

"Peretz is the first and finest work of art that the Jewish people created during this brief period of its secular existence."—Kiev, April, 1917[1]

". . . upon the foundations of earlier aesthetic and cultural values Peretz erected a splendid monument that is the quintessence of our spiritual life. . . ."—Cracow, 1942(?)[2]

"The modern secular Jewish world people began to discover itself in the framework of the new world that was coming into being. Its ideology was in place: Yitzkhok Leybush Peretz was its ideology."—Tel Aviv, 1972[3]

WITH THE EXCEPTION OF Theodor Herzl, founder of political Zionism, no Jewish writer had a more direct effect on modern Jewry than Isaac Leib (Yitskhok Leybush) Peretz. Peretz may not have promoted any fixed political program, but he tried to chart for his fellow Jews a "road" that would lead them away from religion toward a secular Jewish existence without falling into the swamp of assimilation. From the mid-1880s until his death at the beginning of World War I, he shaped literature in Yiddish, and to a lesser extent Hebrew, into an expression and instrument of national cohesion that would help to compensate the Jews for the absence of such staples of nationhood as political independence and territorial sovereignty. He expected that the modern culture of the Jews, embodying the distilled ethics of centuries of religious refinement, would help to sustain the modern people much as Biblical and Talmudic literature and learning had sustained Jews in the past. More by intuition than considered plan, Peretz groped his way toward a politics of culture.

Peretz used the banner word *Bildung,* which can mean both education and culture, to represent the initial phase of his program: the promotion of education in the service of a new Jewish way of life. At first his message seemed not so different from that of the Maskilim, the Jewish enlighteners, who had fought Hasidic influence, championed the study of European languages, promoted the positivist emphasis on productive skills and labor, and substituted inductive reasoning for received ideas. Yet Peretz's sketches and stories and even his editorials could never be contained by their programmatic purpose; his was a richly textured literature in which uncertainty was an integral part. He provided his contemporaries with the vocabulary of their collective experience and the modulations of their individual moods. It was not merely that he wrote about immediate problems and the tensions that strained Jewish families and communities to the breaking point. The intensity and allusiveness of his writing ascribed enduring value to the common inheritance of author and audience, and assumed that they would reach together for a common future.

The comparison between Peretz and Herzl may seem exaggerated to those who are unfamiliar with Jewish communal life between the two world wars. But by the time of his death in 1915, Peretz had attained a towering stature both as writer and national figurehead. If Herzl pointed the way to a national Jewish homeland in Zion, Peretz represented the no less genuine determination of modern Jews to flourish as a minority in Poland, and

Introduction

perhaps elsewhere, with a language and a culture of their own. The Organization of Yiddish Writers in America, founded the year of his death, called itself by his name. In the building that housed the Organization of Jewish Writers and Journalists in Warsaw between the wars, the portrait of Peretz dominated the hall (much as Herzl's portrait became the icon of the Zionist movement). The bibliography of articles and books about Peretz is larger than those of the other two Yiddish classic masters, Mendele Mocher Sforim and Sholem Aleichem, combined. The many schools, streets, landmarks, and cultural institutions named after Peretz in all the cities where East European Jews congregated attest to the vital power of the ideals with which his name is associated. When Abraham Sutzkever, survivor of the Vilna Ghetto, reached Palestine in 1947 and founded what was to become the world's leading journal of Yiddish belles-lettres, he named it for Peretz's drama *Di goldene keyt,* thus evoking its complex vision of the "golden chain" of Jewish succession.

The inspiration that Peretz provided during his lifetime to younger writers and to at least two generations of modernizing Jews continued strong after his death. During the heady days of the Russian Provisional Government in 1917, Jewish writers in Kiev issued a passionate commemorative booklet that opened with Peretz's poem: "Hope! Spring is not far off . . . New birds in new nests will sing new songs. Trust! Night will soon end, and clouds disperse . . . Fresh light, song, aroma will penetrate even our grave . . ." When this poem was sung by Jewish choruses, the music exulted in thrice-repeated "Hope" and "Trust," and almost elided the bitter closing phrase. In general, there was a tendency on the part of the Jewish schools that taught Peretz's works and of the organizations that bore his name to mute the sober undertone of his writing and stress its will to creative life.

The most compelling, and poignant, proof of Peretz's influence came in the ghettos during the Second World War. In the Warsaw Ghetto alone there were at least sixty commemorative gatherings in his name. In the Vilna Ghetto the scholar Zelig Kalmanovitch analyzed one of Peretz's late essays dealing with "whether literature can become the vehicle of the messianic idea." Joseph Wulf began his book about Peretz—a tribute to his style—five months after the occupation of Cracow; one of the eight manuscript copies hidden for him by friends was preserved by the Polish painter Stanisław Klimowski and returned to him after the war by the artist's son. Wulf concluded it with the assurance that Yiddish literature would continue to thrive on the foundations Peretz had established, because he had created his works "under the aegis of eternity."

This monograph attempts to understand Peretz's role in the development of modern Jewish culture—what he wrote and why it mattered. That there has not been a new English study of Peretz in thirty years is reason enough to reexamine his formative influence. But the near eclipse into which Peretz has fallen during the last few decades also prompts a reconsideration of that influence. Peretz's works may well be subject to the inevitable shift of tastes that affects all deceased writers. But he was "more than a writer." His belief that Jews could seek in the *bukh,* the secular text, what they had once found in the God-inspired *seyfer* became, largely through his work and personal example, a new article of faith, almost a new ideology. Now, as this century wanes, and Peretz is hardly

Introduction

known in either Yiddish or Hebrew or English or Russian, the four main languages of contemporary Jewish life, his idea of culture appears to be disproven by the evidence of his reputation. Those who were the core of his readership were annihilated in Europe, but where Jewish life still thrives among their descendants his memory is also fading rapidly. The tens of thousands of Hasidic Yiddish-speaking Jews today use the language as it was used in the premodern age, to preserve their distinctive religious way of life; secular Yiddish writing means no more to them than Shakespeare. The dynamic national culture of Israel in Hebrew no longer accords Peretz a place of honor. And both types of acculturating (or assimilating) societies—the voluntary diaspora of North America and the suppressed diaspora of the Soviet Union—adapt too fluidly to contemporary trends to maintain any "chain" of literary tradition, golden or otherwise.

In other words, both the shattering and the cohesive impulses of history have played their part in the decline of Peretz's ideal of culture. Questions about the legacy of Peretz therefore arise within Jewish culture itself. What were the properties of the literature that proved so inspiring, and were they of merely transitory value? Is Peretz less compelling today because of an aesthetic reassessment, or because of the substance of his thought? The lingering nostalgia of some North American Jews for "Yiddishkayt"—a Jewish humanism that is transmitted through Jewish culture—may benefit from a fresh analysis of Peretz, who best represented this ideal. Lest this attempt of mine to reassess his historical role obscure my devotion to Peretz, let me explain that I am not a Hasidic enthusiast but a skeptical rationalist of Lithuanian stock, and the critical homage of this study is the only kind I consider worth paying.

I. L. Peretz and the Making
of Modern Jewish Culture

Reason and Faith

About the year 1888, Leon (as he was known in Polish) or Leybush (as he was known in Yiddish) Peretz, then a highly successful lawyer in his native city Zamość, was disbarred after being denounced to the tsarist authorities by an unknown informer. Despite his strenuous efforts to clear his name, he was unable to persuade the government to reinstate him. "I fell in battle," he concluded after futile trips to Warsaw and St. Petersburg and equally fruitless appeals to gentile friends in the local court. "I was unable to prove that I was not a socialist, not an enemy of the government, and not hostile to the orthodox church, and that I don't undertake the defense of revolutionary-minded Uniates."[1] The Uniates, who acknowledged the authority of the Pope, were suspected of introducing foreign papal influences into the church, and were thus considered just as dangerous to the tsarist ideal of one national religion as the socialists were to the ideal of one autocratic ruler.

For ten years Peretz had practiced law successfully in the Zamość region, winning high respect for his professional competence. He was admired for his intelligence and learning, and not least for his generosity with money. He and his wife kept an open house for the modernizing young Jews of the town, whom he served as something of a mentor. One of Peretz's friends, Yeshaye Margulis, wondered if his strong influence on local Jewish youth might have provoked some of their orthodox parents to try to drive him from the city for fear of his corrupting powers.[2] Whether or not theirs

3

was the decisive charge, whoever wanted Peretz out of Zamość achieved that purpose. Because he was not given the chance to confront his accuser or accusers, Peretz was never certain who had lodged the complaint against him or why it should have been so decisively upheld. He knew only that at the age of thirty-seven he had suddenly lost his livelihood and had to look elsewhere for a new source of income.

From all we know of Peretz's life in Zamość before this crisis, he seems to have been an energetic, optimistic native son. At a time when a man disclosed his identity in the cut of his beard, Peretz affected the look of a well-to-do Pole; in fact, the stone bust of Count Zamoyski that still stands in the courtyard of the former Zamoyski residence bears him an uncanny resemblance, with its deep-set eyes and thick, drooping mustache.[3] There were many other signs of Peretz's adaptation to Polish society. He conducted the courtship of his second wife, Helena Ringelheym, in Polish, which remained the language of their home. The son of his first marriage, Lucian, who was under his care, he had sent to the larger city of Plock to be educated in Polish. He subscribed to the *Izraelita,* the Polish-language Jewish newspaper, and he even discovered Yiddish literature in a Polish translation. The only works of modern Yiddish literature he seems to have known were Sholem Yankev Abramovitch's *Masoes binyomin hashlishi* (*The Travels of Benjamin III*) and *Di kliatshe* (*The Old Mare*), which he had read in the Polish translations of Klemens Junosza.[4] Peretz had come to maturity during the brightest years of Polish positivism, when faith in universal education, technological progress, and productive labor inspired high hopes of rational human improvement. He was encouraged by the liberal attitudes of the publicist Aleksander

Reason and Faith

Świętochowski (1849–1938) and writers such as Eliza Orzeszkowa (1841–1910) to believe that the Jews would eventually be rewarded for their industry and their loyalty by the respect of their fellow Poles. His personal experience of injustice was not only a severe blow to his pride, and his pocketbook, but to his understanding of himself as a member of the surrounding society. By expelling him from the ranks of lawyers, the tsarist government bureaucracy drove him from the profession that he would probably have practiced to the end of his days.

The year 1888 happens to be famous in the annals of Yiddish literature for another reason. Although the fortunes of the Yiddish press were then at low ebb, the editorship of the single Yiddish weekly newspaper of the tsarist empire, the *Yidishes folksblat* of St. Petersburg, having passed into the hands of a certain Yisroel Levi (who compared Yiddish to castor oil, a necessary purgative), this was the year in which Sholem Rabinovitch launched a Yiddish annual, *Di yidishe folksbibliotek,* that established Yiddish belles-lettres as a major cultural force.[5] Sholem Rabinovitch, better known as Sholem Aleichem, was then still in possession of the considerable fortune he and his wife had inherited upon the death of her father, and he determined to put this money at the service of the new literature by editing a yearbook of high quality. He sent out a call for Yiddish material to well-known Jewish writers in Russia and Poland, promising generous honoraria. Although Sholem Aleichem was still a relatively young man (Peretz's junior by seven years), his address in Kiev, the Ukrainian capital that was outside the Jewish Pale of Settlement, and his respectful attitude toward Yiddish writers and their work promised an improvement over the ephemeral and apologetic character of earlier Yiddish publications. Through a third party, the call for Yiddish material reached Peretz, who at the time had only a modest reputation as a writer of Hebrew.[6]

Peretz had actually begun his writing in Polish. At twenty-two he had produced a small sheaf of poetry in a variety of styles: light satiric verse in the manner of Heine, mildly erotic verse in the manner of Goethe, and fables of the kind he would later compose both in Hebrew and Yiddish. The longest of these maiden poems was on a Jewish theme. The narrator happens upon a tribe of Jews in their airless synagogue during the month of Elul. What is going on, he asks rhetorically. Is the rabbi giving the signal for the onset of battle? Are the agitated Jews embarked on a reconquest of Palestine? No, not at all, comes the answer. When the Jews rise up some day, as they assuredly will, they will not go to war against their enemy but will embrace the brother who had long ago cast his magic spell on them and transformed them into a worm. For the moment, alas, the Jewish worm is still a worm, and the rabbi is merely signaling the beginning of the penitential fast. Here, Peretz's ambivalent attitudes toward both Jews and Christians are clearly in evidence as he tries to balance criticism of religious excess, protest against tsarist oppression, and aspirations of universal brotherhood in a single poem. He was later to dismiss his Polish poems as a false start, an "internationalist moment" that proved alien and had to be abandoned; the Polish manuscript was only saved from oblivion by his relatives, the Altbergs.[7]

His early Hebrew writing did not launch his literary career either. He made his Hebrew debut in 1877 in a small collection of poetry copublished with his father-in-law, Gavriel Yehuda Lichtenfeld, who was said to have supplemented Peretz's limited command of He-

Reason and Faith

brew grammar.[8] By the time the book appeared, Peretz was already divorced from Lichtenfeld's daughter, was about to remarry, and had taken up the practice of law that completely absorbed him for the next ten years. Not until 1886 did he resurface as a writer, contributing poems and sketches to *Haasif* and *Hatsefira,* the leading periodicals in what was gradually developing into the national renaissance of Hebrew as a living language. By then he was also known locally as the author of occasional verse in Yiddish, and it may have been this aspect of his literary reputation that prompted a friend in Berdichev to inform him of Sholem Aleichem's project.

We don't know whether Peretz learned of the new publication before or after he was disbarred; the reference in one of his letters to Sholem Aleichem to the sudden decline in his earnings suggests that he was still trying to win reinstatement. The new literary journal, which Peretz said "surpassed in its significance everything that has been published in both our literatures," was just the sort of project that by harnessing his energies could help offset his humiliation.[9] He could not have considered Yiddish writing a practical alternative to the practice of law, since, as far as he knew, there wasn't a single Yiddish book to be found in all Zamość.[10] The only Yiddish writers then profiting from their labor were the incredibly prolific Isaac Meir Dik, "the first professional Yiddish writer," and sensationalists like Shomer (pseudonym of N. Shaikevitch), whose potboilers Sholem Aleichem held responsible for lowering public standards.[11] But if not an alternative source of income, Yiddish writing provided Peretz with a new creative challenge. His Hebrew works had attracted some appreciative notice among small circles of enlightened Jews throughout the Pale of Settlement,

7

but neither the coterie atmosphere of contemporary Hebrew letters nor the literary resources of the language gave Peretz the scope he apparently needed to develop his social and artistic ideas. With his contributions to *Folksbibliotek,* Peretz began his uninterrupted career as a Yiddish writer—as it turned out, the most influential Yiddish writer of all time.

That Peretz should have taken up Yiddish literature at just the time he suffered a fatal economic and social reversal may be considered symptomatic of contemporary cultural developments. It would be a vulgar simplification to suggest that modern Yiddish literature resulted from hostility to the Jews, but some connection between the two is undeniable. The earlier generation of East European Maskilim had favored the linguistic integration of the Jews into Russian, just as their Central European brothers were learning to function in German. Following the accession of Alexander II in 1855, when the shackles on publishing were slightly loosened, some Jewish writers took advantage of the relaxed censorship to write and publish in Hebrew and Yiddish. But the primary impulse of this literature was exhortation to reform. The enlighteners hoped that political emancipation would mean equal citizenship for the Jews, who would have to demonstrate their readiness for citizenship by adoption, among other things, of the local language. It stands to reason that modern young Jews like Peretz and Sholem Rabinovitch should have aspired to political and social equality; that they chose to educate their children in Polish and Russian, and to speak and write to them in those languages, reveals that their deepest personal hopes for the Jewish future included linguistic adaptation.[12] The particular conditions of Jewish life in Eastern Europe, where a rapidly swelling population was hemmed in by just as rapidly multiplying restrictions, forced the postponement of these hopes. With mixed emotions some Jewish intellectuals were persuaded of the need to develop an independent culture in reinforcement of their separate national identity. In the face of pogroms and xenophobic nationalist tendencies in populist, government, and elite circles alike, they increasingly turned to each other.

Had the process of liberalization that began in Russia in the 1850s maintained its hospitable promise, Jewish creativity would most likely have flowed into the host languages, as it did wherever toleration flourished elsewhere. That potential was never fully realized. In the same way that Peretz rechanneled his energies into writing when his advancement as a lawyer was blocked, on a much larger scale the extraordinary flowering of late nineteenth-century Yiddish and Hebrew literature was a creative response of the Jews to the obstruction of their political progress. Intensified Jewish culture was one spontaneous reaction to social repression. By contrast, those Jews who chose to write in Russian and Polish were forced to confront—in themselves—the growing hostility of those cultures to their Jewish legitimacy.

At the time Sholem Aleichem initiated the *Folksbibliotek,* the status of Yiddish was still much lower among the Polish Jews than it was in the Russian Pale, among other reasons because the political optimism of Polish Jews had been correspondingly higher. Polish liberalism was significantly more hospitable to the Jews than was its Russian counterpart, as long as the Poles expected Jewish help in their struggle for national independence. This proffered friendliness, or expectation of friendliness, held out for a longer time the promise of an integrated community of Jewish Poles.[13] Polish positivism was also immensely encouraging to the Jews. Its emphasis on rational forces of progress, on the need for industrial and technological improvements, on socioeconomic rather than religiometaphysical ideas of nationhood, allowed Jews to consider themselves potential partners in the advancement of the public weal. Yet even before Peretz was disbarred, the public mood had begun to change. The pogrom in Warsaw following the assassination of Alexander II in 1881 shattered the image of Polish-Jewish cooperation that flourished around the time of the 1863 uprising and for a time thereafter. The Catholic Church and the conservative nationalists opposed the accommodationist politics of positivism—the Church because it weakened the religious basis of Polish peoplehood, the nationalists because they still hoped to free Poland from the yoke of foreign rule. From the socialist camp too, there rose an attack on the bourgeois spirit of positivism, which was said to profit individuals at the expense of the working class.[14] The decline in mutual toleration affected the Jews who were at that time being squeezed out of their former occupations by the expansion of industry, a changing peasant economy, the rising Polish middle class, and, not least, discriminatory tsarist edicts. Peretz described this period as the end of the good years and the beginning of the bad. His own setback was typical of the worsening fate of Polish Jewry.

Peretz did more than turn to literature as a result of his dilemma: he turned his dilemma into literature. No longer an inexperienced young man, he took up Yiddish writing with the kind of authority authors normally acquire only after many years of trial and error. Along with his first manuscripts, he sent Sholem Aleichem his credo as a writer: "Your wish and goal (as far as I understand it) is to write for the sake of the audience that speaks jargon of jargon-land; I, for my part, write for my own pleasure, and if I take any reader into consideration, he is of the higher level of society, a person who has read and studied in a living tongue."[15] The letter is written (as is most of the correspondence between them) in Hebrew, which is clearly not the living tongue Peretz had in mind. A paraphrase of Peretz's compressed message would read something like this: though I now find myself writing, as you do, in Yiddish, let me make it clear that I don't consider myself the sort of Yiddish writer you presumably are, adapting your intelligence and your literary style to the market women and the synagogue goers you write about. No, I write for someone as educated and complicated as myself, a reader and student of Polish or Russian, who may also know German and French, and who might now be writing in one of those languages if anti-Jewish hostility had not retarded local Jewish emancipation. "I, who write for my own pleasure and only according to my mood," he wrote, "take my material simultaneously from different worlds."[16]

None of this can be taken as a serious comment on Sholem Aleichem, since it becomes clear in subsequent letters that when he formulated these distinctions Peretz was really thinking not of Rabinovitch (Sholem Aleichem) but of Abramovitch (Mendele Mocher Sforim), and had never read even a word of the author he was characterizing. But it expresses his intentions: he meant to write about himself and the Jewish condition without omitting those feelings and aspirations that put him in conflict with the speakers of the language. His use of Yiddish would not prohibit the investigation of modernity, including its struggle against Jewish tradition and the language itself.

"Monish," the long poem he contributed to the first volume of *Yidishe folksbibliotek,* is just such a work. We can understand why even such sophisticated readers as Sholem Aleichem and the historian Simon Dubnow found it difficult or incomprehensible, because there had never been anything remotely like it in Yiddish:[17]

ir veyst—min hastam—
di velt iz a yam,
mir zenen fish;
(teyl zenen hekht,
shlingen nish-shlekht . . .
zogt efsher nish?)

di velt iz a yam,
breyt on a shir;
di fish zenen mir,
der fisher iz S'M.

The world is a sea
We are the fish
(Some of us carp
Know how to swallow . . .
Don't you agree?)

The world is a sea
Wide beyond measure;
We are the fish
Satan's the fisher.

The work was designated a ballad, but its rhythm was staccato and modern, and the balladeer seemed to be speaking in a language all his own. He joked in Yiddish idiom and dropped rabbinic references like a regular Jew, but was he traditional or not? This world of hungry fish that opened the poem was the universe of Hobbes and Darwin, where our choices are to swallow or be swallowed. But if so, what was Satan—the Satan of the Jewish moral imagination—doing in Darwin's universe? As Satan sets his bait in the next few lines, confident that he will hook his prey, the reader is not really sure whether to trust the poet when he says he has come to warn us against evil, or to recognize him as the devil's own accomplice.

Monish is a prodigy of the golden age of Polish Jewry, modeled, as Peretz was fond of repeating, on himself as a boy, only moved slightly back in time.[18] Handsome and brilliant, Monish is also good and pure, oblivious to the passions he rouses in some of the younger women of the town, unspoiled by the adulation of the great Polish rabbis who recognize in him the future great mind of their generation and perhaps even the "askhalta degeula"—the herald of the Messianic Age. However, perfection is not something Satan can countenance. Warned by a courier demon that this paragon of Jewish virtue may soon put them out of business, Satan plots with Lilith, his female counterpart, to corrupt the boy. No sooner said than done! A wealthy German arrives in town accompanied by his beautiful daughter, Maria, and as the father spoils the community with infusions of easy money, the Christian daughter dazzles the locals with her tantalizingly beautiful song:

> un az monish geyt kseyder
> yedn morgn fri in kheyder
> blaybt er shteyn baym toyer.
> demolt zingt a prakht marie
> un ir treln-melodye
> dringt im tif in oyer!

13

Whereas formerly nothing could distract him from his love of study, Monish now lingers at the gate (*baym toyer*), enchanted by Maria's trilled melody that penetrates deep into his ear (*dringt im tif in oyer*). When he studies, he finds himself repeating her strange new tune. Monish's mother is deeply disturbed when she hears this alien tune instead of the familiar strains of synagogue worship and talmudic study. The tune is a symbol to her of all that tempts a religious Jew into realms of secular beauty and transgression. But the new melody proves irresistible.

Jewish literature contained many stories of such temptation, and the Book of Job had long since suggested that Satan might be provoked by an upright Jew. Peretz personalizes the motif by introducing music—the allure of western culture—as the vehicle of seduction. In early variants of the ballad he goes further: the voice of the "author" intrudes on the action to explain how differently his poem would have sounded had he composed it in a gentile tongue rather than in the Jewish jargon that lacks the vocabulary of love and passion. He ridicules his own attempt to write a love story in a language "smelling of goose fat." (Nor was passion alone missing in his mother tongue; when Peretz began to read philosophic and scientific challenges to religion and felt his faith crumbling, he said he could not even discuss his problem in Yiddish, because he lacked the vocabulary of both the ideas and the doubts.)

Thus it is not surprising that once Monish is captivated by Maria's song, and arranges a rendezvous with her in a deserted ruin, his capitulation is virtually assured. To satisfy the proofs she requires of his devotion he swears by his parents and ancestors, and in ascending order of importance by all the symbols of his religion, including the Torah, and higher and higher, until he utters the name of God—and is struck by the lightning of His rod!

The punishment is swift: laughter in Gehenna. As the demonic orchestra strikes up its merry tune, the devil-kins do the cancan, and Satan and his consort Lilith celebrate their triumph:

> on der zayt fun teyve-toyer,
> bay dem lepl funem oyer
> ongeshlogn, monish shteyt . . .
> s' fayer brent . . . di shpiz iz greyt . . .

Monish stands nailed by his earlobe to the Satanic ark. The fire is hot; the spit is ready. The echoed rhymes of *toyer* and *oyer* remind us at the end that the innocent ear that once listened enchanted at Maria's gate is now nailed to its doom at Lilith's doorpost.

Since Peretz was evidently telling a story of his own "damnation," he could afford an irreverently comic tone. Contrary to the sermonic warnings of his childhood, he knows that one can sin and survive, follow the paths of the Gentiles and prosper, fall victim to Maria's charms and continue as a modern Jew in his native community. His tongue-in-cheek treatment of wily Satan reflects the chutzpa of the modern man who safely transgresses all the old taboos and lives to boast about it.

But from the point of view of that pious world in which Leybush and Monish were so tenderly raised, he was damned in earnest, and beyond appeal. As a boy of fifteen Peretz had discovered European civilization in the form of a private secular library containing the Napoleonic Code, dozens of novels, and books of history, philosophy, and natural law; and what he learned about physics, law, and love transformed him from a yeshiva *bokher* into a modern young man.[19] Now that this educated young lawyer had suffered a humiliating rejection, Peretz was in a position to know how fickle the Gentile could be, leaving him suspended between a world he had quit and one that excluded him. Maybe the joke was on him and damnation meant knowing that hell was the real world where Maria's contempt was his inevitable reward. It would not have been lost on Peretz's readers that being drilled by the ear to the doorpost was the fate meted out by the Bible to the slave who voluntarily relinquishes his freedom. In spite of its playful wit, "Monish" is a painful parable about the makings of the modern Jew out of compounded acts of betrayal—his betrayal at the hands of Maria after he himself had betrayed the Jewish commandments in an attempt to win her heart. Peretz revised this poem more often and over a longer period than any of his other works.

Qualities that would come to be recognized as typical of Peretz were already there in "Monish": the compressed shorthand style that never stops to explain or to amplify; the unfinished sentence, trailing the three dots that became known as the Peretz trademark; the tantalizing mixture of old and new that makes the familiar strange and the strange familiar. Peretz's writing was immediately set apart by its claim of urgency. He was not, like the typical Sholem Aleichem narrator, a raconteur with time to spare, but a troubled man with too much on his mind. Riddled by doubt, he saw everything in dialectical form, every impulse poised against its opposite, every proposition with its challenge. The court from which he had been professionally barred became the recurring seat of his stories, where as prosecutor and counsel, plaintiff and defendant, he represented the warring sides of his own divided mind and heart. In a story of the same period, "Der meshugener batlen" ("The Mad Talmudist," 1890), he dramatizes the interior monologue of a bachelor student who is torn by so many conflicting impulses that he is drawn to suicide as the only way of resolving them all.[20] Peretz occasionally succumbed to such black moods himself.

D isbarment and the loss of professional status had for Peretz serious practical as well as psychological consequences. As a thoroughly modern husband intent on supporting his wife and family, Peretz had to find a new source of income. He appealed to friends and relatives to help him get a job; and when nothing permanent turned up, he took the temporary job of "statistician" for the new research bureau that Jan Bloch had set up to collect information about Jews in towns and villages. One of a select team of researchers, he was sent to the area he knew best around Zamość to investigate the income and occupation, family structure, and military service of the Jewish population. This statistical expedition inspired Peretz's first major work of fiction. Supplementing the knowledge of small-town life he had gained during his years as a lawyer, it gave him material for dozens of literary portraits.

Jan Bloch's project had a good deal in common with Peretz's earlier attempts to clear his good name before the courts. Along with Leopold Kronenberg, his rival for control of the Polish railroads, Bloch occupied a unique position between Christians and Jews. He was one of the richest and most influential men in the country, and his conversion to Christianity had eased his entry into Christian society without obscuring his Jewish origins. This did not trouble him. Bloch shared the liberal conviction of the Polish positivists that any man who expanded industry and commerce, as he was unquestionably doing, contributed to the welfare of a Poland made up of diverse ethnic groups. His continuing wholehearted involvement with the Jews showed how comfortable he felt as a Pole of Jewish descent.[21]

Yet his optimism had been shaken. The Warsaw pogrom of 1881 revealed the presence of popular anti-Semitism, and the threat by tsarist officials in its aftermath that they would extend the repressive May Laws of 1882 to Poland showed what protection was to be expected from ruling quarters. In the mid-1880s Bloch prepared a memorandum on the Polish economy (based on data his own research bureau had gathered) in which he tried to demonstrate the economic contribution of the Jews to Polish society. As anti-Semitism grew more blatant, Bloch initiated a special project to study the economic function of the Jews and to defend them against the mendacious accusations of parasitism. One could say that Bloch was attempting at the national level exactly what Peretz had been trying to do for himself: muster credible evidence that the charges against them were false.

Little wonder, then, that Peretz did not have a good deal of confidence in Bloch's effort. Having but recently been denied a chance to prove his innocence, he knew that facts were an ineffectual weapon against prejudice, and that a scientific survey was not likely to clear persons of the suspicion in which they were held. Nahum Sokolow, the Hebrew writer and activist who helped Peretz get the job and who accompanied him on at least one of the fact-gathering excursions, said they both considered the effort about as useful as fitting glasses to a blind man or cupping a corpse.[22]

Reason and Faith

Nevertheless, both men took the job seriously, and even enjoyed it as something of a diversion from the serious lives they had been leading. To hire a wagoner and set out for a trip of several days or weeks through their home region in order to engage fellow Jews in conversation was highly pleasurable, especially since the two intellectuals had an independent interest in what they were doing. Twenty-five years later Sokolow, by then one of the leading figures of the Zionist movement, described their search for Jewish colonists, tillers of the soil, who would have provided excellent evidence that the Jews were engaging in "productive" labor. Peretz, concentrating on the Jews inside the towns, wrote almost at once his *Impressions of a Journey through the Tomaszów Region in 1890.*[23]

These twenty-two sketches, published in 1891, remain the fullest account we have of the original project, since the rest of the material appears to have been lost when Jan Bloch sent the data in 1898 to Theodor Herzl, who was going to incorporate them in a book-length report.[24]

The *Impressions of a Journey* are distilled reportage. The narrator, a fictional Peretz, travels from the town of Tishevitz, about 17 kilometers from Zamość, to Tomaszów, about 34 kilometers from Zamość, interviewing local Jews and commenting on their welfare. But unlike Peretz, the fictional narrator travels alone, and without interference from any of the local officials we know that the interviewers encountered along the way.[25] Typical of Yiddish literature of this period, the text omits Gentiles to focus exclusively on Jewish society: the narrator takes professional measure of the townspeople, who return his scrutiny with varying degrees of suspicion, curiosity, hostility, and fear.

In fact, the first impressions portrayed are not those

the narrator has of the townspeople but theirs of him. The statistician is staying with an old acquaintance, Reb Borukh, whose house is located alongside the market square, offering a splendid opportunity to eavesdrop on the market women as they discuss his arrival.

A woman says, "That's the one!"

Another says, "Isn't it nice that we poor sheep have shepherds to care about us! But if the Shepherd above doesn't want to help, nothing will help."

A third woman is puzzled: "Can the Shepherd above really need helpers like him?" She is hinting at my trimmed beard and untraditional dress.

More broad-minded, a fourth cites doctors. "Doctors aren't proper Jews, but still and all. . . ."

"That's a different case entirely. A doctor is a private individual. For something communal like this, couldn't they have found a Good Jew?"

Still another opinion is voiced: "Who needs records about us? They should have sent us a couple of hundred rubles instead. Just don't register my son, and see if I care when he doesn't become a shmeneral!"

This is the female chorus of Tishevitz. The first woman, trusting and optimistic, is pleased that Jews have champions of their own—shepherds, she calls them—to look after their welfare. The second, a skeptic, hasn't a particle of faith in the modern reformers— only in God, the Divine Shepherd. The third woman, strictly traditional, suspects anyone who shaves his beard or otherwise deviates from tradition. The fourth, more liberal, points to doctors as proof of the good that modernity can bring. The fifth says, let's not turn the exception into a rule; the occasional doctor may be neces-sary, but our Hasidic faith healers are the real guarantors

Reason and Faith

of life. The last is a simple pragmatist: If they want to help us out of poverty, let them give us money. Her parting shot—see if I care when my son doesn't become a shmeneral!—conveys her belief that increased dangers rather than increased benefits may well be the result of the inquiry.

The masculine counterpart of this women's chorus is a conversation between the host Reb Borukh, who has just finished his prayers, and his guest the statistician, who no longer prays but joins him in a shot of brandy and *lekhayim* at the conclusion of the prayers. The guest is annoyed when Borukh proposes a toast to *Parnoseh*, the decent living that he expects the Almighty to grant him. Why, if he trusts so heavily in God, does he worry so much about the state of his everyday affairs? And why, if he is so concerned for his own affairs, is he prepared to leave the fate of his fellow Jews to God? In effect, he implies that the Jew's faith is hypocritical and self-serving. Reb Borukh patiently explains:

"It's simple. The People of Israel as a whole—that's the Sovereign of the Universe's concern, He bears His own in mind. If such a thing were imaginable, if forgetfulness were possible at the Throne of Glory, there are those who know how to remind Him. Besides, how long can Jewish suffering last? The Messiah *must* come, when we are either all guilty or all innocent. But that's not how it is with the affairs of individuals. Making a living is a different proposition."[26]

Consider the compressed intimacy and the cultural intricacy of these exchanges. We are not surprised to learn that readers had trouble understanding Peretz, and sometimes went to their fathers for explanation. The Aramaic quotation from the Talmud that appears in the original, *mon deyoheyv khayev yoheyv mezoney* (He who gives life also sustains life), the half-finished sentences and phrases, the tremendous reliance on allusive nuance—all required an insider's familiarity with traditional Yiddish that younger Jews, the modernizing ones who read Peretz's stories, had already lost.[27] When Peretz said he was writing for "a reader like himself," he evidently did not mean to translate the traditional part of himself for the convenience of younger moderns, but quite the contrary: to have them recognize, and perhaps regret, the authentic culture they were leaving behind.

The introduction to Tishevitz, in parallel male and female scenes, dramatized the conflict between faith and reason, tradition and modernity, that had been the staple of Haskalah argument. Naturally, Peretz—and his narrator—take the part of reason in exposing such familiar targets of Haskalah satire as the superstitious belief in Hasidic faith healers, ignorance of medicine and science, and religious hypocrisy. But Peretz complicates the argument by putting into the mouths of his traditional Jews a powerful defense and counterattack. The women have every reason to distrust this modern shepherd; their skepticism is not merely the result of intellectual confinement but also of bitter practical experience—experience at least partly shared by the author.

Reb Borukh's defense of what the narrator calls his hypocrisy is equally effective. When the visitor challenges the traditional Jew to choose between all and nothing (either consign your fate to God or be self-reliant, either love your brother as yourself or you are no proper Jew), Reb Borukh remains unfazed. Just because God is the ultimate guarantor of Meaning, He cannot be held responsible for tomorrow's breakfast. Since a man can-

Reason and Faith

not know God's purpose, his faith in the moral order of
the universe can hardly preclude anxiety for the fate of
his own family. In giving Reb Borukh the last word,
Peretz ascribes to him a gritty outlook, intellectually and
psychologically tougher than the narrator's.

The *Impressions of a Journey* brought into Yiddish literature a gallery of vivid characters, such as the frail, el-
derly Skuler rebbetsin who "manufactures" a primitive
kind of soap made from ashes and potato peelings in
order to maintain her financial independence; the moth-
erless little boy who wants God to restore the moon to
its former parity with the sun; the Tishevitz rabbi in his
tattered housecoat, complaining that the town refuses
him the two extra rubles he needs to maintain himself
each week. For all their desperate poverty, these Jews are
sweet and trusting in a way that commands respect not
only for themselves but for the teachings they cite as the
inspiration for their way of life. The most interesting
character, however, turns out to be the narrator himself,
initially a mere observer and transcriber of events, then
increasingly an engaged participant.

By 1890, Peretz was no stranger to the Jewish misery
in the small towns of his district. Years earlier, his legal
practice had taken him to those same Jewish settlements
and exposed him to the same unforgettable scenes of
hardship. For example, soon after he was accredited as a
lawyer, he had tried to collect on a promissory note that
was already long overdue. When he arrived at his desti-
nation with a bailiff in tow, he discovered a bare room
with a solitary couch in it. On the couch lay a tubercular
girl wrapped in rags, who looked at them "as a sheep
watches the approaching wolf." Afterward, when the
girl's mother came home and took in the situation, she
began to howl like a madwoman. Bailiff and lawyer

beat a guilty retreat without waiting for the husband, and the debt was forgotten.[28] The scene, as Peretz described it in a letter to his fiancée, had many of the same narrative qualities we find in the composite *Impressions of a Journey,* written fifteen years later.

The narrator of the travel *Impressions,* a penniless statistician, does not carry young Peretz-the-lawyer's burden of privilege and guilt, but he, too, has qualms about his mission. After he has registered his quota of misery, "waifs next to the geese and ducks in the water at the edge of the swamp; infants in the cradle, crying their lungs out; the helpless sick in bed; boys, hardly more than children, boarding with strangers in order to study Talmud," the statistician loses confidence in his task:

I know in advance that I will find an unlicensed gin mill, a couple of horse thieves, and more than a couple of smugglers.

What will be the upshot of the statistics? Will statistics tell us how much suffering is needed—empty bellies and unused teeth; hunger so intense that the sight of a dry crust of bread will make the eyes bulge in the sockets, as if drawn out by pliers; indeed, actual death by starvation—to produce an unlicensed gin mill, a burglar, a horse thief? . . . Does it know the frequency, strength, or intensity of the heartache suffered by the descendant of an exiled Jewish hidalgo, or of an author of a work on the laws governing kosher slaughter, or for that matter by an ordinary householder, before any of them first did what the law says should not be done?[29]

This questioning is provoked by a Jew of good family who confesses that after three of his four children had died of hunger he had constructed an illegal home distillery to earn some bread for his remaining son. Peretz had

actually discovered in some of the border towns he vis-
ited that many Jews and non-Jews resorted to smuggling
and brewing home alcohol to ward off starvation.[30] If he
were to bring this economic fact to light, the report
would harm those it set out to protect. Moreover, the
facts did not really correspond to the truth. The human
dimensions of this social behavior could not be reduced
to quantified data. If these subjects were to have their
day in court, the imaginative artist would have to sup-
plant the reporter and show that the fate of the Jew is
inseparable from his moral struggle.

This insight begat another. Jan Bloch's expedition,
grounded in material assumptions, sought the ameliora-
tion of Jewish misery through social, economic, and
political improvements. But in effect, the seemingly
rational idea of progress was itself predicated on a spe-
cies of faith—faith in the powers of reason, and on the
good will of governments in applying it. Peretz had
lost his faith not once but twice, and his political skepticism revived in him a dialectical appreciation of traditional belief. Through the eyes of his traveler, he invites us to see that the small-town Jew was not the
reactionary caricature of the earlier Jewish reformers
but a civilized man or woman delicately balancing faith
and doubt—or rather, faiths and doubts—not unlike
his own. Along with the reformist sympathy we might
have expected for the poor and the oppressed, Peretz
expresses in these sketches an intellectual affinity with
ordinary traditional Jews.

After the expedition had completed its task, Peretz
found a job in Warsaw, possibly through the intervention of Jan Bloch, and he moved there with his wife in
1890. From then and until his death twenty-five years

later, he was an employee of the Warsaw Jewish Community Council, an organization that administered public aspects of Jewish life and welfare.[31] Like Franz Kafka at a somewhat later date in Prague, Peretz took advantage of the 9-to-3 working day of a functionary to earn a small steady income while devoting the early mornings, and sometimes the better part of the nights, to his writing. Peretz was a diligent employee. Within a few years he was put in charge of the cemetery section, where as part of his job he had to assess family members of the deceased by determining who was faking indigence and who was too proud to take the charity he needed. Instead of traveling among the Jews, Peretz now had all sectors of Warsaw Jewry streaming in to see him. His friends and colleagues argued over whether this bureaucratic job threatened his creativity by consuming so much of his time and energy, or whether, as his good friend Nahum Sokolow contended, the daily meetings with his fellow Jews deepened his human understanding. Judging from his earlier choice of profession and the many social causes he later espoused, Peretz would have wanted to work with the public—if not at this job, then another.

His move from a small city to the capital offered broader cultural opportunities, though in at least one important respect his social life in Warsaw may have narrowed. The casual access to various levels of Polish society that he had enjoyed in his legal practice around Zamość was missing in Jewish community work. Peretz tried to make up at least some of the loss by keeping up with Polish culture. When he began to put out his own Yiddish journals in Warsaw in the early 1890s, he always included translated selections of Polish fiction that dealt sympathetically with the Jews.[32] This was a way of intro-

ducing Jewish readers to liberal Polish intellectuals, re-
minding them that beyond the repressive regime and the
nationalist anti-Semites there were Poles who believed
in tolerance and even brotherhood. There was also reciprocal interest in Peretz from Polish editors who wanted
to translate his work for their publications.[33] But in the
absence of any integrated Polish-Jewish intellectual circles (apart from the revolutionary movement), a Jew
had to make his choice between the Christian and the
Jewish social spheres that grew further apart as the century drew to a close. Whatever his ambitions of strad-
dling both cultures like a colossus, Peretz had to accept
the limitations of Jewish society, maintaining whatever
literary contacts he could outside it.

In this attempt his aims initially coincided with those
of his employers, well-intentioned Polish-speaking Jews
with benevolent reformist instincts. The targets of their
prescriptive zeal were the Warsaw Jewish masses, swol-
len by the influx of Russian refugees who had been ex-
pelled or provoked into abandoning their homes by the
May Laws of 1882. These so-called Litvaks were poor
but ambitious, and while their arrival threatened the
already-overstrained Jewish economy, it improved the
outlook for Hebrew and Yiddish culture. During the
first months of his sojourn in Warsaw, Peretz tried to
develop a public program under the banner word *Bildung* that aimed to educate the Jews without driving
them from Jewishness. He fought simultaneously on
several fronts: against anti-Semites who charged Jews
with parasitism; against reactionary Jews who resisted
all modern ideas; and against Jews who saw no further
use in Jewish survival.[34]

Peretz's publications of 1891–94 attest to his boundless
energy and intellectual range. To the first volume of *Di*

yidishe bibliotek he contributed the following items: the editorial statement of purpose; an idyll about the affections of a traditional Jewish husband and wife; a translation from the Psalms; a satire of the unmerited respect accorded to a man who had died rich, having no other accomplishments but his wealth; the sketch of a starving Jewish father and child with no food at home to break their Yom Kippur fast; a lengthy discourse on the importance to society of craftsmen and craftsmanship; a feuilleton on the problems of a Jewish writer; a long narrative poem about a wagoner for whom the decline of his business is the end of a way of life; miscellaneous poems; and several items of literary criticism. It was as if he were trying single-handedly to satisfy every kind of Jew: intellectual and worker, female and male, the forward-looking traditionalist and the unassimilated modern. "I am frightened by the sea of our ignorance!" he wrote, trying to explain why he couldn't handle the humor column he had wanted to include in the magazine. A Christian writer could choose to be flighty, because in his open and free world there were some relatively unimportant items that lent themselves to casual treatment. Not so the Jewish writer, for whom everything is either irrelevant or of desperate and dangerous significance.[35]

Peretz may have had Sholem Aleichem in mind when he dismissed the possibility of humor, for there is no doubt that each writer had begun to recognize his antithesis in the other. In appropriating the title of Sholem Aleichem's earlier *Jewish Folk Library* almost verbatim, Peretz had seemed to pronounce himself Sholem Aleichem's replacement, an act of usurpation that helped to poison their relations for many years. Sholem Aleichem, no less concerned for the Jewish masses than Peretz, proposed to lighten the burden of his fellow Jews through laughter. True, the two volumes of *Yidishe folksbibliotek* that he had edited were filled with references to literature as the spice that induces a man to swallow what is good for him, as though he too felt that humorous writing obliged him to justify its redemptive social value. But he regarded entertainment as a sufficient good in itself and distrusted ideological pamphleteering. The consequence of his editorial attentiveness to literature was a two-volume "library" of high artistic merit, higher by far than that of Peretz's publication of almost the same name.

Peretz was more overtly programmatic. He considered humor the kind of indulgence a Jewish writer could not afford, because its impulse was to dissipate anxiety rather than harnessing it to social reform. There were critics— from David Frishman in his own day to Saul Bellow in ours—who disliked the preachiness of his stories and their "Talmudic sophistication."[36] Sholem Aleichem distrusted what he considered the self-aggrandizement of Peretz in assuming a quasi-rabbinic role. Peretz himself seems to have been blinded by his social purpose from recognizing the relative aesthetic merit of his own work. He gave some of his finest fiction the casual label "humoresque" or "sketch," and overestimated stories that show their sermonic underskirts. Writing at a terrific pace, with constant interruptions and distractions, he tried to make his point with force and bite, for readers with no more leisure time than he. Yet Peretz could not always suppress his own doubts in the reasonableness of his reason, and these unexpected little assaults on his own didactic purpose endowed some of his stories with mysterious resonance.

Buried in him, but not far beneath the surface, was a solitary man with powerful feelings who yearned for things beyond the attainable. Although the schedule of a public servant and the literary mission of a public reformer left little room for impracticality, Peretz was sometimes tormented by unrealizable ambitions and dreams. He appeared to crave not only romantic associations with women, but in literature, too, an outlet for restlessness and loneliness and desire—isolating sensations that he had felt since boyhood. This is the mood that permeates many of his lyrics, and the stifled longing finds its way into some of his stories.

"When times are bad even Torah—that best of merchandise—finds no takers." This crisp opening sentence of the short story "Kabbalists" (Hebrew, 1891; Yiddish, 1894) leaves little question about its materialist bias.[37] The folk expression *"toyre iz di beste skhoyre"* (Torah is the best merchandise) urges Jews to regard Halakhic study as more valuable than any other pursuit. Peretz the modern writer turns the teaching around to say, Torah is no exception to the economic pressures that govern society. Jewish proverbs notwithstanding, when times are bad, yeshivas decline.

There follows apparent confirmation of this economic principle:

The Lashtchever yeshiva was reduced to Reb Yekl, its master, and an only student.

Reb Yekl is a thin old man with a long disheveled beard and eyes dulled with age. His beloved remaining pupil, Lemekh, is a tall thin young man with a pale face, black curly earlocks, black feverish eyes, parched lips, and a tremulous, pointed Adam's apple. Both are dressed in rags, and their chests are exposed. Only with difficulty does Reb Yekl drag the heavy peasant boots he wears; his pupil's shoes slip off his bare feet.

Reason and Faith

Concentrating on physical detail, Peretz compresses into a taut opening paragraph all the relevant background for his story. Since the decline of once-thriving yeshivas could be observed all over Poland, readers would appreciate the contextual "realism" of which these two figures were but an example. Economic hardship means Jews neglect the yeshiva; the hunger of teacher and student leads to sleeplessness, and insomnia arouses in them a desire to delve into the mysteries of Kabbalah. The spiritual quest of Reb Yekl and his student Lemekh is rooted in their deprivation. Physiology determines mysticism: "as long as one has to be up all night and suffer hunger all day, let these at least be put to some use" in fasts, and self-flagellation, and the pursuit of mysteries.

But once having set the scene, Peretz lets us hear for ourselves the voices of the two Jews as they study Kabbalah together. "The melody that requires words," the rabbi explains,

is of the lowest order. Somewhat higher degree is the melody that sings of itself, without words, sheer melody! But this melody too requires voicing, lips to shape it, and lips, as you realize, are substance. No matter how refined, sound itself is still a substance.

Let us say that sound stands on the border between substance and spirit. But in any case, that melody which is heard by means of a voice that depends on lips is still not pure, not yet authentic spirit. The true melody sings without voice, it sings within, in the heart and bowels.

This is the secret meaning of King David's words: 'All my bones shall recite . . . ' The very marrow of the bones should sing. That's where the melody should reside, the highest adoration of God, blessed be He. . . . This is part of the melody with which God created the world; it is part of the soul which He instilled in the world.

This is how the hosts of heaven sing. This is how the rabbi, of blessed memory, sang.

The rabbi is heaven-bound. While the narrator trains our eyes on the body, Reb Yekl is reaching for the realm of spirit so pure that all trace of material necessity has been eliminated. Starving, neglected, the teacher and student speak a sacred language of mystical striving that repudiates the narrator's focus on their grubby feet. And the student is even more refined than his teacher. When a rich man's servant brings the rabbi some food and Lemekh experiences a momentary pang of envy, he punishes himself with a penitential fast that weakens what is left of his starved body. In his final hours, trained on the quest for heaven's light, he reaches higher and higher until as he expires he feels about to enter the realm of unadulterated spirit, "pure melody":

The entire town was unanimous in wishing such a death for themselves. Only the master of the yeshiva was unsatisfied.

"Only a few fasts more," he sighed, "and he would have died with the Divine Kiss!"

Of course, the narrator controls the story, and the conclusion brings us sharply back to his point of view. The same harsh voice that began by impugning the town's reputation now ends with proof of its hypocrisy and bad faith. Had the pious Jews of Lashtchev really wanted such a death, they could have starved themselves instead of neglecting to feed the student. As for the teacher, his final judgment verges on humor. There is a well-known Jewish joke about a wagoner who trains his horse to eat progressively less and less and then complains, when the animal drops dead one day, "What a

Reason and Faith

shame! I had almost gotten him to go without food altogether." In the yeshiva master's disappointment that his pupil did not reach the ultimate Kabbalistic height of being brushed (like Moses) by the lips of God, the narrator echoes the absurdity of that joke. The reader is meant to know the difference between spiritual transcendence and dying of hunger.

Peretz knew that reason was not to be denied. The Jews as part of humankind had to learn the laws of nature and analyze the structure of society in order to improve their common lot on this earth. The material component of spiritual behavior was for Peretz a given, and neither in this early story about Kabbalists nor in his later writings did Peretz waver in his humanistic convictions: Lemekh should have eaten and died hereafter. Yet Peretz admired Lemekh's idealism, perhaps more than his own reasoned wisdom, and he allowed Lemekh's yearning to permeate the story as it irradiated his life. Lemekh, who reached "higher and higher" in pursuit of his own moral vision, was the antitype of Monish the betrayer. In defying the limits of his flesh, Lemekh also cut into the Haskalah satire that had no use for his martyrdom, and into the materialistic outlook that scoffed at the love of God.

Hebrew may have released in Peretz yearnings with which the language had eternally been associated. In Hebrew he wrote not only the first version of "Kabbalists" but also of "Mishnas Hasidim" (Hebrew, 1894; Yiddish, 1906), the prototype of his later neo-Hasidic tales.[38] This extended mood-piece has none of the ambivalence of the earlier story, but frankly exults in the power of emotion over reason:

Talmud scholars with all their shallow knowledge are like visitors to the king's palace who have the pleasure of seeing it from the outside but cannot enter. . . . But those truly immersed in the Torah, whose souls cleave to the Torah, enter the palace, they see the full glory of the King, they hear the songs of praise to the King, they become one with the whole before the King.

Hasidic storytellers customarily expounded their mystical teachings in the language of majesty; Peretz brings it to his readers at second hand. Through the voice of a disciple of the departed Rebbe of Nemirov, the story describes how the true religious ecstatic had once danced at the wedding of his only daughter, with the joy of one who has penetrated the "palace of the king." The disciple testifies to the spiritual attainments of the Hasidim in days gone by, to the lesser grandeur of Jewish intellectual faith embodied in the Rebbe's Lithuanian son-in-law, and to the subsequent falling off from those heights. By substituting the Hasidic narrator for a modern narrator like "himself," Peretz can go much further than he did in "Kabbalists" in admitting luxuriance of spirit. Starved for the faith that he had lost, Peretz had discovered a way of admitting into literature the yearning for divinity without its content, the theme of spiritual striving without responsibility to the object of that striving. A modern story might set off reason against faith so that it did not have to accept the limitations of either.

In the 1890s Peretz became the dominant cultural figure of Polish Jewry. His modern treatments of traditional life gave the illusion that a natural transition was possible from the religious, small-town communal life of the past to the secular individual strivings of young Jews in the cities. His works were the language in which this process could be charted and discussed. Monish was

Reason and Faith

the Jewish Everyboy who had to risk even damnation because of his overpowering attraction to the siren song of western culture. The traveler through the Jewish towns of the Tomaszów region—a Monish grown somewhat older and wiser—rediscovered the value of the world he had left behind in the course of exposing its precarious decline. His adventures warned against the overhasty move from traditional faith to "progress," which depends for its implementation on untrustworthy governments and questionable theories. Stories of Kabbalists and the Hasidic faithful pointed similarly in two directions. Now that the authority of the yeshivas and the Hasidic courts was collapsing, their alumni might acknowledge how much they owed to the God-centered past. Coming as they did from the man who insisted on the modernization of the Jews in every sphere, from physics to politics, these works argued by their very form that Jews should take along as much of their baggage as possible in their passage from home, and travel forth as the children of their parents. Peretz showed in his person how it could be done.

Nation and Class

Elul is a month of worry, of serious contemplation and heavy heart for the young man in a small town who is still stuck body and soul in the world of religion. In Elul there occurred the great rupture. . . . It happened to me quite suddenly. In the morning the seven heavens were still suspended above me. . . . by evening it was all over. I realized that there was no point in trying to shore up the structure wobbling on feet of straw, and let it fall like a pile of rotting timber. My former self remained buried under the ruins.[1]

HERSH DAVID NOMBERG was here describing the great crisis of his life. At age eighteen, the son of a respected Hasidic family, he was already married and the father of a child, living according to the custom of those years under his father-in-law's roof so that he could more assiduously devote himself to Torah, when his sudden loss of faith undermined all his habits and assumptions. If he doubted the existence of the Jewish God, he could not pretend to serve God's purpose through marriage, procreation, study, and daily observance. For someone of Nomberg's spiritual sensitivity, living *as if* he still believed was impossible. So he accepted the consequences of his enlightenment, began to educate himself in Russian, separated from his wife and child, and took up the lonely drifter's life that he later captured so effectively in Yiddish stories.

Yet already at the moment of crisis, Nomberg tells us that he discovered at least one solace. During the same penitential period of 1894 when he lost his belief, a friend gave him a copy of a book of verses in Hebrew,

Haugav (*The Harp*), that had just appeared in Warsaw. "I read the poems, reread the poems, and involuntarily began to sing them aloud," he wrote. The love lyrics in this slender volume had moved him to tears. In a musical language echoing Biblical and ancient Hebrew, Peretz had expressed his sense of loss for something irretrievable and—as in this poem "The Date Palm"—a yearning for comfort and assurance that will never come.

> Hagidi li, timoyro,
> madua yofuakh
> ruakh tugo kharishi
> al shadmas habriyo?
>
> Ha'im loy nafshoys meysim
> yishpkhu es rukhom,
> es yeyush horikovoyn
> el koys leyl haksomim?
>
> Hagidi li, timoyro,
> haumnom yokum novi
> uvevikas hoatsomoys
> ya'ase nifloysov?

(Tell me, little date palm, why does the sultry wind of grief blow across the earth? Have not the souls of the dead poured their putrid despair into the cup of enchanted night? Tell me, little date palm, will a prophet appear to perform his miracles in the valley of dry bones?)[2]

Nomberg was touched by the singularity of this Hebrew poetry that expressed uncertainty and pain so much like his own. From the shattered foundations of the religious past they had in common, this poet had

38

rescued precious images that bound him to others, dispossessed like himself. Nomberg's first impression of Peretz was formed from the dignified and somber portrait on the inside cover of this little book of poetry. Three years later, when he was brought to Warsaw by a network of young enlightened Jews who sponsored provincials like himself, he paid his first shy visit to Peretz's home to show him his own Hebrew verses. Peretz rewarded his admirer by advising him to switch to Yiddish so that he could be of more practical use to his fellow Jews. Despite this ambivalent reception, Nomberg became a frequent guest in the great writer's house, one of the many young men to start his literary career under Peretz's guidance.

It is impossible to exaggerate the influence of Peretz on the development of Jewish culture during his twenty-five-year sojourn in Warsaw. There is hardly a writer or intellectual of the period who did not leave an account of Peretz's influence—from Joseph Klausner, the passionate Zionist and unswerving Hebraist who was Peretz's neighbor for three years, to Shakhne Epstein, Bundist turned Communist and later Soviet spy, who recalled that the first illegal assembly he attended in Warsaw was a lecture by Peretz about the development of religion.[3] Among those who made the pilgrimage to Peretz's home at the start of their literary careers were Sholem Asch, Sh. Ansky (Rapoport), Joseph Opatoshu, David Bergelson, Bal Makhshoves (Dr. Eliashiv), Itche Meir Weissenberg, Yekhiel Yeshaye Trunk, Yehoash (Solomon Bloomgarten), Ephraim Kaganowski, Alter Katsizne, Der Nister (Pinkhas Kaganovitch), Abraham Reisin, and Lamed Shapiro, to name only the most prominent figures of Yiddish literature.[4] Almost all of these young men had experienced an upheaval like Nomberg's that left them looking for an alternative source of authority or inspiration, or for at least a new cultural direction. In Peretz they found a willing guide. Peretz was not content simply to write in Yiddish and Hebrew and to hope that his work would be translated into Polish and Russian. He wanted to shape a whole new Jewish public, a modern Jewish people. Since he could not do this without the enthusiastic assistance of the younger generation, he needed the fledgling writers as much as they needed him.

Everyone agreed on the extent but not the nature of Peretz's influence. Hemmed in by the confines of Jewish Warsaw, he was always restlessly seeking something new in the thought and writings of other nations to broaden his own intellectual and artistic horizon. If he was fatherly—both encouraging and reproachful—to the many aspiring writers who came to see him, it was at least in part because of his hope that one of them might offer him some fresh idea or untried theme. Throughout the 1890s his reputation grew among admirers and critics; and the critics may have done even more for his name than the admirers. Serious opposition to his writings, which gave them a measure of notoriety, suggested that a cultural movement was consolidating among young Jews as a result of his influence.

We have seen what Peretz was for Nomberg: a poet who could transpose the Jewish passion for holiness into a secular context. By contrast, the writer and playwright David Pinski knew Peretz as a political idealist, one of the key figures in the growth of the Jewish labor movement just prior to the founding of the Socialist Bund. When Pinski came to call on Peretz during his first Warsaw visit in 1891, he made no connection between the Peretz whose poems he had read in the He-

brew periodical press and the Peretz whose short fiction
had just begun to appear in Yiddish, never imagining
that the Hebrew romantic poet and the Yiddish satirist-
realist could be one and the same. Having come to call
on the Yiddish Peretz, he was expecting to find a young
man like himself, and was taken aback by the stocky
figure about his father's age who answered the door.
But Pinski soon fell under Peretz's spell, "an enchantment," he was to write forty years later, "from which I
never freed myself and never wanted to free myself."⁵
For three years he worked alongside Peretz, putting out
a series of publications that maintained their external
Jewish form while introducing the ideas of class consciousness and socialist thought to many levels of the
Jewish reading public.

Because the government would not give them permission for a regular Jewish periodical, Peretz and
Pinski adopted a local publisher's idea of putting out
holiday issues; since there was hardly a Jewish month
that did not have one holiday or another (and even
Sabbath could serve in a pinch), the publication would
be a monthly in fact. Under the guise of marking a
holiday, the editors promoted their ideas and tried to
disseminate useful information. Seventeen issues of
Yontev bletlekh (*Holiday Pages*) appeared from Passover
1894 to Purim 1896. Along with Peretz's other publications of the mid-1890s—the miscellany *Literatur un lebn*
(*Literature and Life*) and the third volume of *Di yidishe
bibliotek*—they were the most radical Yiddish publications of their time, excepting only the illegal pamphleteering of revolutionaries. During this period when the
nascent labor movement was beginning to organize its
workers' circles using the Jewish vernacular as the language of agitation propaganda, Peretz's publications

were valuable tools. The writer Sholem Asch described a moment during the celebration of Peretz's literary anniversary in 1901 when a delegation of workers came to present him with an inscribed, worn copy of his *Yidishe bibliotek* that had been passed around the Warsaw prison from cell to cell.[6]

P eretz's enthusiasm for what he called "the new movement" taking shape in Western Europe was part of the same program of *Bildung*—education through acculturation—that he had undertaken many years earlier in Zamość. It meant exposing the Jewish public to the latest European advancements in science and culture. Some of this adult education assumed particular urgency, as when, during the epidemic of 1892, Peretz issued a booklet explaining that *He Who Doesn't Want To—Needn't Die of Cholera*. The lengthy articles he wrote about air, magnets, and other principles of natural science for every issue of his magazines were meant to improve the attitude of the Jews to their environment, so that new inductive habits of mind should engender healthier habits of hygiene. With the same intention of encouraging improvements in the social sphere, he tried to present socialist theories to his readers using the informal language of sketches, parables, short stories, and didactic essays. The introduction of these concepts proved far more complicated than the teaching of natural science. Censorship imposed limits on the promotion of socialism, but an even greater constraint was his own ambivalence about dogmatic social theory and the international world order that it championed. His uneasy attempt to balance nation and class resisted any fixed political idea.

Take a story called "The Miracle of Chanukah" that Peretz wrote for the Chanukah issue of the *Yontev bletlekh* of 1895. Its narrator is an impoverished Jewish intellectual who supports his ailing mother by tutoring the children of the Warsaw Jewish bourgeoisie. When the tutor arrives one Chanukah afternoon at the brightly lit Berenholc home for his weekly lesson, his pupil balks at having to work on a holiday, and to avoid his ordeal he invites the tutor to join the family at the table for tea. There sit three generations of the Berenholc family: the rigidly observant grandfather; the slightly modern traditional son; and the two children—the pupil and his older sister, who is absorbed in a novel.

Over tea, the pupil mischievously provokes a discussion about Chanukah during which the tutor is asked to explain the meaning of the holiday. Torn between fear of losing his job if he reveals the extent of his freethinking, desire to impress the young woman with his own ideas, and a need to teach the truth, he extols the armed struggle that the Maccabees waged for Jewish national independence while condemning the wealthy assimilationists of ancient Judea who tried to ingratiate themselves with the Greeks. But he leaves out the supernatural part of the story: the miracle of the Temple oil that burned for eight days though it barely sufficed for one.

His tightrope act elicits two responses: first the daughter of the house stops him in the hall to ask whether he is against assimilation.

"Assimilation," I answered, "means to eat, to consume, and to digest. We assimilate beef and bread, and others wish to assimilate us . . ."
"Then will there always be wars and conflicts among nations?" she asks after a frightened silence.
"Oh no," I reply. "At a certain point all nations will have to unite!"
"As what?"

"Humanity! . . . if each nation acts as it ought to, then all will all come together on common ground."

At this point their conversation is interrupted, never to resume. The following day the tutor receives his second response in the form of a ten ruble note from Berenholc, terminating his employment.[7]

Undistinguished, certainly, this story dramatizes the author's ideas, which are as tangled and equivocal as those of his hero. He exposes the reactionary and hypocritical elders without outright condemnation of the festive practices that still serve his national ideals; he damns the Jewish bourgeois father, but only for firing a tutor who is not teaching what he was hired to teach; he upholds the universalist standard of a united humanity, but renounces assimilation as a means of achieving it. Small wonder that given so many contradictory impulses, all that finally impresses itself on the text is the sickly, unstable condition of the narrator, who resembles many other despairing antiheroes of contemporary fiction. Peretz's contributions to these pages frequently betrayed a battle fatigue that was quite at odds with their inspirational purpose.

Peretz also wrote less ambiguous stories, striking out at explicit targets and abuses. "Mendl Braynes" (1891) and "A kas fun a yidene" ("A Woman's Rage," 1893) excoriated traditional culture for placing full material responsibility on the shoulders of the Jewish woman while assigning to males only the weightless moral burden of study.[8] This division of labor gave unscrupulous husbands the religious sanction to enslave their wives. In the first of these stories a man gets credit for his good deeds while his wife sacrifices herself literally to the bone for his material comfort; in the second, a nursing mother is driven to the

Nation and Class

threshold of suicide by the smug refusal of her husband to combine his Torah study with any support of her and the baby. Alert to the women's issue that had been on the reformist agenda at least since the publication of the Russian radical critic Nikolai Gavrilovich Chernyshevsky's *Chto delat'?* (*What Is To Be Done?*) in 1864, Peretz dramatized the torment to which weary seamstresses and youthful brides were subjected at the hands of employers, parents, and in-laws. Peretz's attraction to women expressed itself not only in love lyrics and intermittent romantic adventures, but through his lifelong championing of many aspects of the women's cause.

Peretz was particularly clever in his assault on religiosity that uses piety as a camouflage for exploitation. In this he was building on Haskalah satire, perhaps the only branch of Hebrew and Yiddish literature that can be said to have had a long and impressive tradition. Peretz's story "The Shtrayml," attacking the rabbinic fur hat that governs the Jews, irrespective of the fool or knave who wears it, armed a new generation with fresh anti-Hasidic ammunition.[9] His fable of "The Pious Cat" that always manages to kill the bird became a byword for religious hypocrisy that finds ever more unctuous justification for throttling its victims. A piercing sketch called "A Destroyed Sabbath" showed how quickly the idyll of Jewish marriage could be destroyed by the religious laws that claimed to be protecting its sanctity. When a mother insists that her daughter refrain from sexual relations with her husband because of the merest hint of the onset of menstruation, she kills the joy of Sabbath and the young couple's pleasure.[10]

Whatever fears Peretz had about assimilation, he never doubted that the Jews had to absorb the latest theories and findings of Western Europe, and he was certain that this higher knowledge would translate into moral improvement. Nothing angered him more than a reissued quasi-scientific work like *Sefer Habris* by Rabbi Pinchas Hurwitz of Vilna, which purported to educate its audience while it actually trotted out old superstitions. "If there were such a creature," writes Peretz about a kind of lizard that supposedly emits a fire-quenching spray when you throw it into the fire, "say, here in Warsaw, why no one would ever get as much as three rubles [of insurance] out of a fire!"[11] He appealed to the reader's common sense to defy folk zoology and Creationism, because Judaism should not have to be protected under the banner of ignorance.

To some extent, Peretz followed the example of Yiddish forerunners and contemporaries by introducing new ideas in traditional language. This sound pedagogic strategy and familiar Haskalah device gave his writing the illusion of cultural continuity. The Dubno Maggid, one of Poland's outstanding Jewish preachers, had spent some years in Peretz's native city of Zamość, and although several decades separated the two men, it is hard not to see in the modern secular *maggid* a transmutation of his sharp-tongued religious predecessor. Indeed, transmutation was a favored device of Peretz's; by tracing a family or a melody through several metamorphoses in time and place, he demonstrated the varieties of cultural evolution.

Yet Peretz was also intent on disturbing the reader's peace, on forcing change. Unless the traditional mind could be dislodged from its habitual path, the story would not have served its purpose. Caught as he was between the conflicting desires to prove the usability of the Jewish past and to promote urgently needed reform, Peretz sometimes tipped the emphasis to one side, sometimes to the other. The pace of change, however, was independent of his will. As carefully as he weighted his stories, their internal balance was to shift when the changes in Jewish life outstripped his intentions.

An example of this tension between the radical and the conservative impulses, "Bontshe shvayg" ("Bontshe Be Silent"), became, almost from the moment of its appearance in 1894, the most famous of Peretz's stories.

Here on earth the death of Bontshe Shvayg made no impression. Try asking who Bontshe was, how he lived, what he died of (did his heart give out? did he drop from exhaustion? did he break his back beneath too heavy a load?), and no one can give you an answer. For all you know, he might have starved to death.

The death of a tram horse would have caused more excitement. It would have been written up in the papers, hundreds of people would have flocked to see the carcass, or even the place where it lay. But that's only because horses are scarcer than people. Billions of people![12]

Bontshe had passed through this world like a shadow, without uttering a word of complaint. All the descriptions of poverty and misery of Peretz's urban reportage came together in the figure of this poor wretch who had been abandoned in infancy, raised without any tenderness or concern, abused in succession by stepmother, father, employers, wife, and child, and whose place in the charity ward when he dies is claimed by twenty others like him.

But to the same degree that the earthly tribe ignores him, the heavens celebrate his arrival with a hallelujah chorus. From the highest angels to the cherubs, from Father Abraham to the Godhead itself, the Jewish paradise welcomes Bontshe into its amplitude. Convinced that there has been some mistake, and terrified of what

47

will happen when he is discovered, the object of this adulation gradually realizes the life being presented to the heavenly court by the defense counsel is his own. The defense counsel expends unnecessary energy trying to stir up sympathy for the poor victim, because the prosecutor concedes the case. He tells the court simply: "Gentlemen, *he* kept silent. I will do the same." Bontshe's earthly travail was so great that his final judgment is mere formality. The heavenly judge pronounces the verdict in a voice like a harp, and so the story ends:

"My child . . . there, in the world below, no one appreciated you. You yourself never knew that had you cried out but once, you could have brought down the walls of Jericho. You never knew what powers lay within you. . . .

"The Heavenly Tribunal can pass no judgment on you. It is not for us to determine your portion of Paradise. Take what you want! It is yours, all yours!"

Bontshe looked up for the first time. His eyes were blinded by the rays of light that streamed at him from all over. Everything glittered, glistened, blazed with light: the walls, the benches, the angels, the judges. So many angels! He cast his dazed eyes down again. "Truly?" he asked, happy but abashed.

"Why, of course!" the judge said. "Of course! I tell you, it's all yours. All heaven belongs to you. Ask for anything you wish, you can choose what you like."

"Truly?" asked Bontshe again, a bit surer of himself.

"Truly! Truly! Truly!" clamored the heavenly host.

"Well, then," smiled Bontshe, "what I'd like most of all is a warm roll with fresh butter every morning."

The judges and angels hung their heads in shame. The prosecutor laughed.

Can there be any doubt of the story's political thrust? In the figure of Bontshe, Peretz challenges the ideal of goodness that had a powerful grip on the folk imagination. So you think that passive goodness in this world will be granted divine recompense in the world beyond? That suffering can be compensated by some transcendent moral scheme? Very well, then, let's play out the heavenly drama as generations of Jewish preachers have taught you to imagine it. There is your Bontshe, the exemplary sufferer, a Job without even the impulse of rebellion. Upon leaving this world of illusion he goes straight to the true world where—as promised by perfect justice—he receives the supreme reward. Everything works schematically as it should, except that this creature is beyond redemption. His soul is too meek and his outlook too narrow to make possible any ultimate restitution. Bontshe's failure to develop a character in the material world destroys any chance of postponed spiritual life. The moral scheme that makes a hero of Bontshe is itself morally flawed.

Bontshe's silence in this story about speech means that others must seek justice on his behalf. After his appropriately noisy reception in heaven—to make good his whispered existence on earth—his case is put forth by a glib lawyer who appeals to our social conscience and weaves a rhetorical spell to capture our sympathies for the victim. Yet it is the prosecutor who has the last laugh, because a man who does not know his worth cannot be granted worth, and must remain eternally worthless. All the liberal sympathy in heaven and earth, including the liberal sympathies of an author like Peretz, can't do for Bontshe what he is too passive to do for himself.

The judge's observation that Bontshe might have brought down the walls of Jericho had he only exercised his legitimate right to complain, comes too late to save him, but perhaps not too late to save Peretz's readers. One can see how profitably such a story was used by early organizers of the Jewish socialist movement who in fact complained of the chronic passivity of the workers. They reported that the Jewish workers whom they tried to radicalize were thoroughly fatalistic, responding "as God wills" or "as God grants" to all inquiries about their conditions.[13] To make such workers recognize the flaw of Bontshe in themselves was the first step in teaching them to demand their due.

Yet for all its tendentiousness, this transmuted folk legend struck an unexpected chord in its modernizing audience; despite the story's explicit opposition to Bontshe's passivity, his sweetness apparently reminded readers of the old values of humility and moral containment. The times soon began to exert their influence on the text. The tempo of change as the nineteenth century neared its end was so rapid that it overtook all those who were promoting rational schemes of progress. Emigration, like a tidal wave, kept gaining strength toward the end of the century, and eventually swept three million Jews to North America and thousands more to Argentina and Palestine. The revolutionary movement, programmed by Marx and Engels for the industrialized and emancipated West, found unexpectedly fertile ground in the tsarist empire, where the absence of a strong independent middle class made it easier for one group of political dictators to replace another. The revolt against Jewish tradition which took the form of flight from the shtetl was no longer a story of a handful of defiant youngsters, as during Peretz's adolescence, but of thousands and even tens of thousands.

Nation and Class

In such an atmosphere of massive dislocation, many readers looked to Jewish literature—*their* literature—for stability rather than innovation, for the kind of spiritual compensation that Nomberg had found in the Hebrew verse. In Bontshe they recognized the pitiable casualty of the Jewish past, and because they suspected that there would be no room for him in their future, they felt some affection, even nostalgia, for the man whose highest aspiration was a buttered roll. The familiar Jewish cast of the story seemed to contradict its revolutionary theme, showing Bontshe as suffering saint, a holy fool, the Jewish martyr. Later, as the actual number of Jewish victims began to climb, in the pogroms of 1902–5, the First World War, the 1930s, and finally, in the destruction of European Jewry during World War II, the benign interpretation of Bontshe became almost irresistible, and the story entered the canon of literature inside out. When my mother says, "Ikh vil dokh nit mer vi Bontshe—a heyse bulke mit putter" (I don't aspire to any more than Bontshe—a hot roll with butter), she is invoking a model of humility.[14]

If the fictitious Bontshe could not be contained within political boundaries, how much less so the real Peretz. He was especially problematical to the organizing socialists who tried to assess whether he was ever a true radical and which stories could best be harnessed to their cause. Spontaneous at first, this need to label Peretz became urgent when ideology hardened into dogma, and Soviet Communism required that the permissible Peretz be separated from the condemned. To facilitate their task, many socialist critics isolated the mid-1890s as the "radical period of Peretz's writing," trying to find at least one programmatically reliable point in his oeuvre. They based their judgment on the phraseology of such passages as these:

. . . we believe emigration is useful only inasfar as the emigrant wishes to exchange trade for labor; to exchange yard goods, scale, and dry measure, . . . living by tricks, lies, ruses, for earning a living by the sweat of his brow; inasfar as all those suspended between heaven and earth by a spider's thread of "God will provide" want to find permanent work with a secure future.[15]

During the mid-1890s when Peretz associated with David Pinski in Warsaw, and wrote for the socialist press of London and New York abroad, he sometimes sounded like the committed Marxist editor and writer Morris Winchewski, who even complained that Peretz was plagiarizing his work.

A full-blown biographical legend about Peretz developed in tandem with these scattered texts. Police raids on suspected revolutionaries often turned up copies of the *Yontev bletlekh;* according to the literary historian Nachman Meisel, a search of Peretz's home on the night of May 17, 1895, though it uncovered no evidence, cemented the author's reputation as a radical. Four years later Peretz was finally arrested.[16] On July 30, 1899, at a public meeting that was advertised as the celebration of an engagement, the real "bride" and "groom" of the evening, Peretz and Mordecai Spector, read from their works, donating the proceeds of the evening to the workers' cause. Peretz had agreed to participate at the invitation of two young women, who at first pretended that they were raising funds for their families' travel to America, but then under his scrutiny confessed their actual purpose. It was rumored that Peretz had decided to appear at this illegal assembly despite warnings of an impending police raid.[17] The three months that he subsequently served in Pavilion Ten of the Warsaw Citadel (the same prison where the revolutionary Rosa Luxemburg, also a native of Zamość, later served time) rounded out this irresistible portrait of the Yiddish literary colossus who contributed his authority to the proletarian cause at the very moment of its consolidation.

The episode of imprisonment can also be looked at quite differently from a nonhagiographic perspective. The gathering on July 30 was one of many semilegal meetings that Peretz addressed during these years, and only the accident of his arrest gave it special prominence. The incident even took a comic turn when in their search for a revolutionary, the police initially picked up Peretz's son Lucian, who looked the part more than his father did. When the real accused was finally arrested and imprisoned at the beginning of August 1899, he served his term with Mordecai Spector, the same man who had quit the *Yontev bletlekh* four years earlier because he disagreed with its too-strident socialist tone. According to Spector, far from courting imprisonment, he and Peretz had agreed to appear at the workers' rally only upon assurance that the evening was kosher (i.e., had been granted police approval). Spector, who had been imprisoned twice before, quipped that there wasn't a Jew in Russia who had not done time in a tsarist prison; the police net was stretched so thin in those days that it often caught the minnows while permitting the big fish to slip through the holes.[18]

Peretz's cultural affinity with the radicals never amounted to political affiliation. His approach to reform was idealistic rather than ideological, based on a vision of better human beings rather than on a scheme for their improvement. Even as he continued to contribute to socialist publications and to draw attention to social injustices, Peretz made it abundantly clear that he distrusted the divisive class impulse of socialism as much as he relished the dream of a kindlier international world order, and that he feared the leveling instincts of egalitarianism as much as he opposed the exploitation of urban workers. He felt comfortable in workers' and students' circles only as long as they were still groping for direction (though even then he was aware that he did not really speak their language), but once the movement acquired an organized political mandate it filled him with dismay.[19] To Yehoash (Solomon Bloomgarten), who moved to America in 1900, he wrote that he would not rush to save the proletariat: "I seek in every movement a moral base. The proletarian movement has such a base, but doesn't want to acknowledge it."[20]

Peretz seems to have assumed the role of moral instructor even in the most lighthearted situations. To celebrate the holiday of Purim in the first year of the new century, the Yiddish and Hebrew writers of Warsaw decided to congregate at an all-night masquerade party. Following a student costume procession representing the successive stages of Jewish history from Egyptian slavery through the contemporary *chalutz* movement, Peretz was asked to distribute the traditional Purim gifts, the *shalekh-mones,* as he saw fit. He gave a magnet to the members of the Jewish community council "so that they should be drawn closer to Yiddishkayt"; a match and some straw to those who claimed they wanted more Jewish "warmth"; bitter almonds to the editors whose excessive sweetness had been causing diabetes; and so on. He was at least moderately dissatisfied with every segment of Jewish society: with the nationalist enthusiasts for their treacly sentimentality; with the acculturated Jews for their distance from the nation; with the socialists, too, for throwing over the spiritual traces of their heritage along with its religious observances.[21]

A few years later, the revolution of 1905 was to turn Peretz even further away from radical politics. He was dissatisfied with the philosophical and psychological implications of socialism, not only with its applied revolutionary tactics. He bridled at the materialistic emphasis of Marxism, much as he had rebelled against the statistical methods and premises of Jan Bloch's expedition a decade earlier. "There will be no empty stomach," he wrote in 1906, warning socialism of its future, "but souls will go hungry. . . ."[22] As the ideological basis of socialist movements hardened, they in turn repudiated his critical independence and unfairly accused Peretz of capitulating to tsarist conservatism.

Whereas in typical revolutionary biography the prison term is the "university" that completes a radical education by hardening the prisoner's political resolve, Peretz's three months in prison seem to have completed his move in the opposite direction. If we are to believe Spector's testimony, Peretz began writing neo-Hasidic stories during this prison term, and they were immediately published in the periodical Der yid. Perhaps he reached for the spiritual reassurance of a neo-romantic literature in reaction to the limitations that prison routine forced on his freedom and comfort; or else this period of incarceration, in the last year of the nineteenth century, quickened a process that was already under way.

For a number of years Peretz had been trying to impress on his followers the importance of gathering folk materials—the stories, songs, and sayings of ordinary Jews that were as important to the creative life of a people as the formal works of their writers. Inspired by Polish ethnographers, some of whom showed great appreciation for Jewish folklore, this interest served at least three ends: it reinforced the ideological shift of attention from the Jewish intellectual aristocracy to the common folk; it strengthened the claim of Jewish cultural distinctiveness (as the Poles, Ukrainians, and Germans have their folklore, so we have ours); and it provided an inexhaustible source of fresh literary material and inspiration.[23] We have already noted how Peretz's respect for the intellectual and religious refinement of the provincial Jews muted his reformist zeal. The concentration on folklore expressed and intensified his appreciation for the *creative* achievement of ordinary Jews, which could serve their writers as both source and inspiration. At the turn of the century Peretz began to adapt some of these folk motifs in a series of works he called *folkstimlekhe geshikhtn*—stories in the folk manner.

Linked to this was his reappropriation of Hasidism. Not that Peretz ever dropped his opposition to the Hasidic dynasties, their miracle-working rabbis, their faith in the supernatural, or their reactionary policies. Peretz's greatest Yiddish interpreter, Shmuel Niger, is certainly correct in inviting us to differentiate between "hasides" and "hasidish"—between, on the one hand, the author's continuing dislike of Hasidism and, on the other, his discernment of certain vital, "democratic," and spiritual elements within the Hasidic movement that could be put to artistic use.[24] Like his stories in the folk manner, so too these stories in the Hasidic manner shaped an imaginary past that could provide an enriched moral basis for the Jewish present.

Several of Peretz's best-known Hasidic stories were published in the pages of the Polish Zionist weekly *Der yid*. Founded in 1899, two years after the first Zionist Congress was convened by Herzl in Basle, this remarkable publication (first a bimonthly, then a weekly) set out to encompass all Jewish interests, by which it also meant the interests of all Jews. It tried to maintain, against factional tendencies within the Zionist movement itself and the splintering of Jewish political parties outside it, an ideal of national unity that refused to surrender any part of the people—not the traditional Jew nor his antitraditional rival, neither capitalist nor socialist, neither the impulsive colonist who wanted to build the Jewish future in Eretz Yisroel nor the family man who was content to fulfill his Zionist obligation by paying his shekel and reading *Der yid*. Although most of the paper was devoted to political analyses, it also featured literature born of the same expansive national feeling, none more so than Peretz's stories with Hasidic motifs.

Until then Hasidim and Hasidic courts had represented to Peretz as to most Haskalah writers a premodern, obscurantist element in traditional Jewish society. Indeed, at the same time and in the same periodical that Peretz published his tales in the Hasidic manner, he continued to excoriate the real Hasidic leaders who still ruled their small-town flocks. But now he also began to find in the social sympathy of Hasidism for the ordinary unlettered Jews, and in its metaphysical yearning for a taste here on earth of the ecstasy of God's presence, a metaphor for his own struggle. Moving backward in time to the beginnings of the movement, he used Hasidic materials more as legend than social reality, the legend of the soul's rebellion against materialist reductionism. In "Between Two Mountains" ("Tsvishn tsvey berg"), one of his most ambitious stories based on Hasidic motifs, he represents this struggle through the clash between a great Talmudic scholar, the Rabbi of Brisk, and his former pupil the Rebbe of Biale, who leaves his teacher because he finds the world of Halakhic scholarship too narrowly elitist and spiritually arid. The Talmudic ideal of Brisk reveals itself to the student Nahumke in a dream as a glittering palace, the walls of which—when he reaches out to touch them—are really made of ice. From this privileged and lonely grandeur, Nahumke flees to the ordinary Jews to reinvigorate them with vital faith. His ability to inspire enthusiastic belief wins him renown among the simple folk and finally convinces his former teacher, the Rabbi of Brisk, to stop his persecution of Hasidic believers.[25]

A craving for glory inspired the author in writing this story as much as it did the Hasidic rebbe in teaching his followers to seek God through joy. Rather than put down one combatant at the expense of the other, Peretz presents the conflict between the rationalist and the ecstatic through the eyes of a disciple who reveres the learned Rabbi and adores his holy Rebbe. Both sides of the Jewish inheritance—its civilizing legal demands and its liberal compassion—are characterized with appreciation for their grandeur of mind and spirit. It was as though Peretz, after too many years of exposure to rational social theory, tried to release his dammed-up faith by evoking those who still possessed theirs.

Critics recognized that these neo-Hasidic stories were part of the general neo-romantic trend in European culture that likewise reacted against a surfeit of realism and rationalism by reaching for transcendence at second hand. A few readers, then and since, have found them hollow; Nomberg, who had been so enraptured by Peretz's earlier Hebrew romantic verse, thought that they captured only the costume of Hasidism, not its spiritual core.[26] Peretz himself expressed his envy for the writer M. I. Berdichevsky, who, having grown up among Hasidim, knew them authentically and at first hand.[27] Most of the stories make no attempt to conceal the critical intelligence that is monitoring the achievement of Jewish mystics and ecstatics. Because the narrators of these stories, even the purported Hasidim among them, do not invite suspension of disbelief, readers who yearn as genuine Hasidim do for the transcendent will feel cheated by the humanistic application of motifs of faith. Yet Peretz did something remarkable in the stories on folk and Hasidic motifs: he alerted his contemporaries and the next generation to the mythic and spiritual resources in their indigenous culture as well as to the potential sterility of modernity should it lose those resources. Together with the resurgence of political will, Peretz inspired an introspective Jewish literature that drew from deep religious roots.

Peretz's relation to political Zionism was no less qualified than his loyalty to socialism; and in the same way that he tried to extract from socialism its moral impulse while resisting its political determinism, so too he tried to harness the national optimism of Zionism, in its first decade as a movement, without accepting its geographic implications. Between those who sought a political solution for the Jews *dortn*, there, or *do*, here, Peretz was always firmly among the *doistn*, those who insisted that there could be no Jewish future at the expense of the Jewish here-and-now, the Yiddish-speaking mass of Polish Jewry. The establishment of colonies in Palestine he considered a hopeful prospect for the youth who settled there, provided they did not pretend to offer a political alternative for the entire Jewish people.[28] Peretz was by no means prepared to surrender to Ahad Haam's vision of a new spiritual center in Eretz Yisroel, because he already felt himself to be at the spiritual center of a viable Jewish people in Poland.

What the burgeoning Zionist movement did provide, particularly in its first still fairly unified period, was a new national self-confidence. There was an upsurge of Hebrew publishing that brought young Hebrew writers to Warsaw. Just as every new Yiddish paper tried to recruit Peretz for its pages, so Hebrew writers tried to involve Peretz in their literary projects, encouraging him to translate his works into Hebrew and to resume Hebrew writing more vigorously.[29]

This renaissance did not necessarily imply an optimistic or chauvinistic literature; the Hebrew writings of some of those who shared the Zionist ideal, like Chaim Nahman Bialik and Yosef Chaim Brenner, were exceptionally bleak and harsh. When Peretz served as one of three official judges for the short story contest sponsored by the Warsaw newspaper *Hatsofe* (*The Spectator*), first prize was unanimously awarded to I. D. Berkowitz for "Moshkele Pig," the account of a boy who reacts to brutal mistreatment at the hands of his father and Jewish officialdom by transforming himself from Jew into Gentile.[30] Bialik's most famous poem, *Be'ir Hahareyga* (*In the City of Slaughter*), written after he had been sent by the Jewish Historical Society of Odessa to interview the survivors of the pogrom in Kishinev in 1903, presented a shocking indictment of Jewish passivity in the face of massacre and degradation. Yet the direct appeal in the poem to the *missing* national dignity, to the absent God and the broken will of what should have been a mighty people, generated a determination to rise to the challenge of its accusation.

Peretz reacted very strangely to Bialik's poem. After its appearance in Hebrew, Peretz published a Yiddish version so weak that Sholem Aleichem accused him of intentionally sabotaging the text, and a miserable Bialik felt obliged to rewrite the poem in Yiddish himself. Klausner tried to defend Peretz, claiming that he had tried to pass off his modified version as a newly discovered Byronic "Hebrew Melody," because they were both certain that in its original form it would not satisfy the censors.[31] But this would not explain why Peretz should have tried to translate it in the first place. He was obviously disturbed by the poem. Bialik's bold prophetic treatment of the pogrom subject went further than any previous work in recognizing the massive political threat of anti-Semitism and the incapacity of Jews to confront the danger. Whether the poem was read as a call for local self-defense or for national resettlement in Palestine, its animalistic images of the pogromists and their slaughtered victims did not presage the kind of local coexistence that Peretz championed and in which he desperately wanted to believe. Instinctively, Peretz may have wanted to protect himself and his fellow Jews from the force of Bialik's vision by diminishing it and tempering something of its pessimism. If so, he acted less out of the petty jealousy of which he was accused than out of much deeper fear that a literary work of such obvious merit would threaten his own vision of the Jewish future.

Peretz was sufficiently inspired by the renaissance of Hebrew to attempt a major Hebrew work himself, a drama parts of which Bialik considered "sublime," despite its marked difference from his own tragic vision.[32] Peretz's work also challenged the Jewish will by dramatizing Jewish weakness, but strictly within the spiritual sphere. While in publicistic columns and feuilletons Peretz acknowledged the growing threat of political anti-Semitism, he avoided almost all reference to it in his poems and stories, reaching back instead to exclusively Jewish themes of a bygone past. *Khurbm beys tsadik* (*The Destruction of a Hasidic Dynasty*) treats a larger epic subject than he had ever attempted, the decline of a Hasidic dynasty and the spiritual pauperization of the community it had once tried to invigorate.

For all his effort to break new literary ground, Peretz still mired the first Hebrew version of his play in Haskalah clichés. At its center was the tragedy of Feygele, granddaughter of the Hasidic rebbe, who is punished by her grandfather for falling in love with a freethinker, and incarcerated in the cellar of their house. The ensuing loss of faith and disintegration of the rabbinic dynasty results from this initial travesty of religious zeal. The play's action was highly contrived (with voices issuing from the cellar to suggest the buried sins of the household), and none of the characters came to life.

Not until he began reworking the play in Yiddish did Peretz realize its potential. Like Bialik's *City of Slaughter*, the full-length drama that eventually emerged from his labor, *Di goldene keyt* (*The Golden Chain*), became the most nationally significant, if not necessarily the best of Peretz's works.[33] Instead of attributing the decline of faith to a repressive religious leader—an accusation as exaggerated as the grandfather's treatment of Feygele in the Hebrew version—Peretz tried to penetrate the mystery of Messianic belief and its ambiguous effect on the Jews. He continued to portray the Hasidic leader as irascible and stubborn, but in this new version Hasidic passion through the generations manifests itself in a struggle with God rather than in prosecution of the Law.

As the scene opens late Saturday night in the Rebbe's chambers, the Hasidim who have come to spend the Sabbath are agitated and puzzled. Shloyme, their tall, very dignified spiritual leader, refuses to end the Sabbath by making Havdalah; and unless he brings the Sabbath to an end, they cannot go home to their workaday affairs. What will happen to their shops if they cannot return on time to business? And what will happen to the world if the Rebbe defies its God-given order?

Reb Shloyme's refusal to end the Sabbath is no idle whim. Year in and year out he has witnessed the Jewish reality:

> The people . . .
> Two, three, four,
> Five little minyans
> Of little, little Jews . . .
> Wasted,
> Withered
> Little Jews . . .
> Humpbacked they come
> To knock at the Rebbe's door . . .
> Frozen little souls,
> Little hearts,
> They come to stretch their hands
> To the eternal flame:
> Give us a spark! A spark!
> A trickle of alms,
> A little miracle,
> A sign, a wink from the beyond . . .

And each is for himself
For his wife, his child,
His household only. . . . (Pause)
And here, between death and life,
A world hangs in doubt!

To release the heart of the world that is drowning in its blood, Reb Shloyme decides to force God's hand. Against the prescribed order of the calendar and the anxious wishes of his followers, he determines to hold on to the Sabbath at all costs. He will transform his miserable congregants and himself into Sabbath Jews— festive Jews with souls aflame, who dance and sing over the ruins of this world on their way to Him, to God who fashioned them in His image. Once they reach the seat of glory, they will no longer plead or grovel but stand upright, the great proud descendants of Abraham, Isaac, and Jacob, who would wait no longer but came toward the Almighty with the Song of Songs on their lips. Shloyme's image of these stalwart Jews appearing confidently before their God repudiates the Jewish icons of passivity, from the silent Bontshe to Bialik's desecrated victims.

Inevitably, Reb Shloyme's vision of glory is forced to yield to the little aspirations of little men, and the rest of the play is a study in decline. The frantic Jews persuade the Rebbe's son Pinkhas to take over his father's author- ity by making Havdalah in his stead. Pinkhas com- mands a defensive position, willing to sacrifice the masses as long as a few followers are prepared to uphold the strict discipline that he equates with Jewish dignity. Pinkhas's son Moyshe is too weak either to storm the heavens or to enforce his will on those on earth. By the fourth generation it looks as if the golden chain of tradition will snap. Yoynesn, part visionary like his great-grandfather Shloyme, and part disciplinarian like his grandfather Pinkhas, seems absorbed in his own private world of mystical dreams, while his sister Leah (a later version of Feygele) has defied the reactionary darkness of her family to run off with a doctor in search of the light. By the end of the play a humbled Leah returns. The child she bore in the fullness of scientific light turns out to be blind. Looking into its eyes, she knows that only the spiritual illumination of her family will bring back the child's vision. She comes home to beg her father to grant her child sight at the very point when the old man is losing the last vestiges of confidence in his spiritual powers. Yet his beadle, named for the people, Israel, refuses to let the dynasty die, and when Reb Moyshe declares that he can no longer lead the congregation, Israel names Yoynesn the leader in his stead. The play ends in near pandemonium, with the Jews trying to convince the boy to assume dynastic leadership. His sister Leah adds her voice to the plea. Before the curtain falls Yoynesn pronounces his first decisive words, "I am"—we will never know whether with true or forced conviction. In place of the visionary Jewish rabbi who was once prepared to force God to his purpose, a straggle of Jews now tries to shore up some authority from below.

This play—mixing history, legend, and symbolism—provided modern Jews with a cultural vocabulary. A confirmed socialist argued that the play was as much about their movement as it was about anything Jewish: the Hasidic dynasty was an artistic metaphor for the waning spirit of every modern movement that begins in great idealism and eventually deteriorates into disciplinary regulation to compensate for its weakening resolution.[34] In essence, however, by turning from the dimension of space to the dimension of time, Peretz was also turning inward, away from worldly conflict to what had once been the struggle of the Jews with their God and was now increasingly the struggle of the individual Jew with his conscience. All the pressures that were turning the Jews into the diminished and frightened creatures of Reb Shloyme's description, of which the pogroms were only the most violent example, remain extraneous to the drama, leaving only the vertical conflict between Father or fathers with sons. To be sure, the distinction between *hasides* and *hasidish,* between genuine religious impulses and their metaphoric adaptation, also applies to this family drama that probes the psychological problems of succession in the modern age. In another sense, however, by interpreting history as an exclusively Jewish, and largely moral progression, the play maintains the illusion of an autonomous Jewish developmental process, limited by personal shortcomings and national failures alone.

When we consider that Peretz's followers used to serenade him with the Hasidic melody, *Undzer rebenyu,* we may be sure that the play also referred to his own burden of leadership. Responsibility to the Jews, disillusionment with the blind limits of enlightenment, and mourning for the lost messianic faith are recurring themes for Peretz, who inspired his modern congregation less by quelling than by voicing their doubt.

Peretz complained of the difficulty he had in shifting scenes and locations in his fiction; this may help to explain why he never attempted a novel. If the action had to be interrupted and moved to a different place, he had trouble keeping the thread of the narrative.[35] The unities of time, place, and action (broadly understood) alleviated this problem in the theater, which offered the kind of direct access to an audience, the emotional immediacy that Peretz treasured in art. Nevertheless, for some people, Peretz the man always remained greater than any of his works. "We thought that out of his mighty inner conflict he would give us *Faust;* instead he became Faust,"[36] was the judgment of David Bergelson, one of the most gifted prose writers of the younger generation, who felt that Peretz splintered his genius instead of consolidating it in a single effort.

In his bleaker moods, Peretz may have concurred with this assessment. He provided his own unforgettable image of the Faustian bargain in his fable of the billygoat. Once upon a time the horns of this billygoat had been endowed with magical powers; extended to their full length they could catch a star, and ask the star to remind God of His promised redemption. In this way the billygoat was an inspired link between the Jews on earth and their highest aspiration. But one day a poor Jew discovered that from a piece of the billygoat's splendid horns he could carve himself an unusual little box of snuff. Other Jews were not long in claiming the same for themselves. The billygoat granted so much to so many that his truncated horns no longer extended to the heavens.[37] A man of great capacities cannot simultaneously concentrate on a sublime goal and meet the demands of so needy a people. The burden of leadership grew heavier as these demands increased.

C learly, literature was for Peretz part of a much larger undertaking. Like the lawyer whose professional success depends on his ability to protect his client, he wanted his writing to secure the Jews—from the accusations leveled against them by the tsarist government and growing sectors of the population, and from the consequences of mounting despair. He composed his most ambitious works for the Yiddish theater after the ban against it was lifted in 1905.[38] Jews who had already developed the habit of attending the Polish theater and the informal garden theaters now began to flock in large numbers to performances in their native language, and Peretz was among the first to try to harness this form of popular entertainment to larger national aims. He was always looking for possibilities of national self-expression; and as he had surrounded himself with young radicals when he was trying to educate the public through his little magazines in the 1890s, so he now tried to interest young followers in the prospects of a national Jewish theater in Warsaw. He hoped that the Jewish theater and such related projects as a Jewish chorus and music society could unite the Jews without isolating them from their neighbors. Indeed, the Jewish theater might also attract educated Poles, in much the way that Jews were drawn to Polish theater, and impress upon them how culturally advanced the Jews had become.

Unlike the competing national or socialist ideologies, culture was not necessarily confrontational. If his play about a Hasidic dynasty were performed in a Warsaw theater, it should not threaten the Polish playwright whose drama had been performed there the night before, but perhaps inspire him to attend the Jewish performance to see what they might have in common. Peretz himself had done many translations from other languages, especially Polish, and he rejoiced that some of his works had been translated into Polish for Jewish and non-Jewish readers. The *Hazamir* organization he helped to establish for the spread of Jewish music; the People's University that he sponsored and under whose auspices he lectured;

the development of a Yiddish theater that preoccupied
him for the last decade of his life; the cultivation of a
variegated literature—these were for Peretz not simply
arenas for personal self-expression but the cultural foun-
dation upon which he hoped a modern Jewish people
could realize its destiny.

The twenty-five years Peretz worked as a Jewish civil
servant for the Warsaw Jewish Community Council coincided with an urgent search for a new basis of modern
Jewish existence. The simultaneous consolidation in 1897
of Zionism and Jewish Socialism—as well as the appearance of Simon Dubnow's *Letters* that set out the terms of
Territorialism—shows how eagerly, one might say fran-
tically, the Jews of that time were looking for a solution to
the problems posed by their secularization on the one
hand and the rise of anti-Semitism on the other. The
modern Jew who could no longer be contained in the
ghetto—or, for that matter, easily distinguished from
non-Jews—was proving a far more serious threat to
many European nationals than his bearded and caftaned
coreligionist who still observed Jewish practice. Modern
Jews, for their part, once having quit their religious affiliation, had to find both a political and a psychological alternative to the religious identity of the past. Peretz, who
continued to press for the future of Jewish life in Poland,
sought practical answers to the dangers of assimilation
and anti-Semitism, both of which attacked from without, and of the self-doubt that bored from within.

How then, if not through a national homeland or a
socialist international, could the modern Jewish people
redefine itself as a viable and unthreatening group? More
by instinct than anything else, Peretz groped his way
toward a politics of culture, taking for his model the
Poles among whom he intended to remain. He imagined

a Jewish people parallel to the Polish people, sharing the same national soil, and producing an equally rich modern culture in its own languages—Yiddish and Hebrew. No more than the Poles could deny their affinity to Catholicism could the Jews deny the religious dimension of their identity. He thus drew liberally on religious themes and subjects for his modern stories and plays. No more than Polish socialists were ready to sacrifice their national cohesion should the Jews redefine themselves exclusively along class lines. Opposition to assimilation was the most consistent feature of Peretz's politics between 1890 and 1915.

With modern writers and intellectuals taking over the moral leadership from rabbis and preachers (the same way Polish writers and intellectuals were taking over the authority of priests), Polish Jews would constitute an autonomous national community alongside the Christian Poles. Jews and Poles would develop complementary cultures and cultural institutions on a common soil. It may seem paradoxical that Peretz's resistance to assimilation had as its ultimate goal the legitimation of the Jews as part of Poland. Yet to Peretz this was no paradox. Anti-Semitism precluded assimilation because it discriminated against the Jews. Jewish nationalism opposed assimilation because the Jews were a distinct group in the family of nations. The Jews had to prove themselves worthy to others by becoming socially and culturally worthy to themselves.

Hope and Fear

WHEN Peretz began to write his autobiography at the invitation of the periodical *Yidishe velt* in 1913, he told his readers to expect a key to his works rather than to himself.[1] Confessional self-exposure in the manner of Jean-Jacques Rousseau remained restrained in modern Hebrew and Yiddish autobiography, and while Peretz was prepared to mine his personal life for clues to his development as an artist, he did not altogether intend to defy his culture's idea of decorum.[2] The first scene he describes, of being recognized by his parents in early childhood as an *ilui,* an intellectual genius, would not have been out of place in rabbinic hagiography. Peretz locates his beginnings as a Jewish public figure in that discovery of himself as a prospective scholar-sage.

Naturally, his parents tried to tailor an education to his special needs, a task made more difficult by the boy's restlessness and the scarcity of good teachers in the region. Neither locally nor among the rabbis in neighboring towns who undertook to tutor him did he develop sound habits of study. But in any case, a curious boy such as he, raised in the cosmopolitan atmosphere of Zamość in the latter half of the nineteenth century, would have rebelled sooner or later against the limited Jewish curriculum and way of life. The decisive step in his transition from designated Jewish scholar to secular modern occurred when a certain Michael Fidler, who had tried to open a local lending library, offered the boy a key to his storehouse of books so that he might read there whenever he wished. Peretz called this his initiation into *their beys medresh*—the gentile house of study. At age fifteen he began reading European novels, works of history and philosophy, natural science, and the Napoleonic Code of Law. This exposure to the fruits of western civilization made him avid to learn more. Finally came the day—inevitable in Jewish biographies of the period—when he borrowed money from a sympathetic acquaintance, arranged for a driver to wait under his window before dawn, and prepared to set off for university.

But if the memoir is a key to Peretz's writing, the door it opens at this point is virtually astonishing:

The carriage is ordered, I pack in greatest secrecy. Earlier than usual I pretend to go to bed, my sack under my pillow, knowing that I will not close my eyes. A whistle from the street is to be my signal. I put out the lamp and take my leave of everyone and everything in the dark house; my heart is not entirely easy . . . but I must . . . Lying there I hear a soft rustling in the next room. I listen. My door softly opens. Quietly, in bare feet, my mother enters. I barely see her by the pale moonlight through the window. She moves softly toward the bed, sits down at the foot of it, looks at me with pain in her face. I cannot shut my eyes. I must see her and go on seeing her, as the tears run softly from her eyes . . . She is saying goodbye to me. . . . Who gave away my secret?

But she is on guard over me, her tears are on guard over me. . . . I don't leave.[3]

Thus the most dynamic Jewish writer of his generation, the man credited with having single-handedly created a Jewish nineteenth century,[4] presents himself in the story of his life as a youth who could not tear himself away from his mother's love. Peretz offers no further explanation for this decision to remain at home, nor any hint

Hope and Fear

that several years later, under different circumstances, he did go on to study law. The silent exchange between mother and son stands as climax of his autobiography. Its first consequence, the marriage that immediately followed to a young woman his father had chosen for him (with every reasonable expectation of his happiness), is merely the denouement, the unraveling of a plot that had already been resolved. Compared with the romance for which his reading and imagination had prepared him, his arranged marriage was a humiliation, and Peretz claimed not even to have remembered in which town it took place. Within a few years and two children, one of whom died in infancy, the couple was divorced, and Peretz took charge of their young boy. The decisive encounter of his memoirs is not between the young man and his bride but the earlier one between the young man and his mother, in which moonlight and tears, the stage props of romance, are introduced in the name of filial devotion. Peretz presents himself as the forever loyal— or forever captive—son.

The fact is, Peretz really did stay home, and the emphasis of the autobiography alerts us to a side of his character that his great fame otherwise obscured. Opposing the ceaseless adventurism of his mind was a powerful centripetal force. After he became a lawyer he settled into practice in his native city, and had he not been deprived of his professional license he probably would have continued in local practice for the rest of his life. He talked of emigrating to Argentina in the early 1890s and of visiting Palestine in 1909, but he never seriously made the effort to go to either place.[5] Instead, he stayed in the same job for twenty-five years, and turned his Warsaw flats, first on Ceglana Street and then on Jerozolimskie, into a literary home for all. Of the recognized giants of Yiddish literature (along with Mendele Mocher Sforim and Sholem Aleichem), though he alone is considered a modern, he traveled the least, never leaving tsarist territory until he was fifty-one, and then only for a rest cure prescribed for his health. Apparently his readers complained of his lack of knowledge about the globe, because he apologized to them in one of his columns for the geographic mistakes they accused him of making: "Maybe I am guilty because actually—I don't know geography and that's why I never offer advice about where to go. . . ."[6] His well-advertised and lifelong sensitivity to "Litvaks"—Jews who came to Warsaw from the east—suggests an aggressive provincialism that gives instinctive credit to what is most familiar.

Peretz's unusual friendship with Jacob Dineson may also be considered in this light. Dineson made no secret of his adoration of Peretz from the first moment he met him in Warsaw in 1890 to the years after his death, when he asked for and received from the widow Helena Peretz permission to be buried beside her husband in her stead. There was always much amused and tender speculation about this lonely bachelor who suspended his own literary career in order to be at the constant service of his superior colleague. But the other side of the friendship was no less fervent. When Dineson left Warsaw in the early 1890s, Peretz begged him to return. He would welcome him "as a bridegroom greets his bride."[7] Dineson without him was a zero, he said, but he without Dineson was zero minus. The domestic language the two men used between themselves was not unusual in Jewish literary circles (Sholem Aleichem and Mordecai Spector also addressed one another playfully as husband and wife), and if the modern mind immediately associates such usage with homosexuality, it is clear from their complete lack of self-consciousness that these Jewish writers did not. His friendship with Dineson meant that Peretz had not only one motherly wife in Helena, who had no children of her own, but a second literary consort in Dineson to oversee the details of his literary career.

Whereas most contemporary autobiographies introduced the generational conflict through the tension between fathers and sons, Peretz's identification of his mother as the parent from whom he must win his independence allowed him to emphasize the strong filial bond that remained intact rather than the intellectual ties that were ruptured. Gorky's writings, which gave such prominence to the mother as the life force of Russian civilization, may have suggested to Peretz a similar indebtedness on his own part, albeit within a very different civilization. Peretz's hushed mother by moonlight conveys something of the legendary mother Rachel, weeping for her children as they pass by her tomb into exile. She is kindly and compassionate, a human manifestation of the *shekhina*, the female emanation of God, who brings him spiritual grace while exacting from him a certain reciprocal responsibility. A passionate believer in the freedom of the human will, Peretz interpreted his decision *not* to leave home as the determining moral choice of his formative years, the decision that governed his life as a writer.

In thus exposing the emotional roots of his intellectual life, Peretz was coming to terms with perhaps his deepest source of conflict. He had long since feared that his manhood could be gained only through intolerable acts of betrayal. In one of his earliest stories, "Venus and

Shulamith," two boys in the study house, like two warring voices inside the writer, debate the relative virtues of erotic and sublime love. Chaim, the naive Jewish boy, has never heard of Venus, to whom his friend Selig compares his beloved Hannah. Deriding Chaim's ignorance, Selig describes the tempestuous love goddess of Greek mythology, and likens Venus to the heroine of the Song of Songs. Now it is Chaim's turn to be indignant. How can a vengeful adulteress and murderess be compared to Shulamith, whose love is stronger than death? "Rivers cannot carry it off, the sea itself cannot extinguish it." Why, Shulamith is so chaste that she regrets that her shepherd-lover is not her brother, for then she might have kissed him. Carried away by the splendor of Shulamith, who is also the image of the Jewish people in love with their Almighty God, Chaim refuses any comparison at all: "Let your Hannah be compared to whomever you like; to Miriam with her timbrel, to Abigail, to Rehavah, to Delilah, even to Queen Esther; but not to Shulamith! No one can be compared to her, absolutely no one, do you hear?" The story ends with this fervent defense, though it is obvious that irresistible European culture is out there waiting.[8]

In this innocent sketch Peretz shows us the spontaneous connection between erotic and intellectual desire, and the crisis into which it plunges the studious Jewish boy. At least initially, at the point of being led into temptation, the choice between Shulamith and Venus, between an arranged marriage and a quest for romantic love (or, as Monish experienced it, between the study of Torah and the song of Maria), forced a practical decision between staying home and spurning one's home. Peretz recognized how much was at stake in this youthful deci-

Hope and Fear

sion, and how unbearably great was the sacrifice of either alternative.

The filial temper is the ascendancy of son over lover, and Peretz explored the indissoluble links of body and mind in facing this choice much as D. H. Lawrence was to do some years later. He felt the tension between erotic freedom and creativity, not only as it affected the Jew or the artist but civilization as a whole. Concurrently with "Venus and Shulamith," he wrote a lighthearted sketch about the Chelmites, the inhabitants of Jewish foolstown, who decide to rid the world of the *yeytser hore,* the evil impulse of lust, by ensnaring him, burning him to a crisp, and scattering his ashes to the winds. Their success has unanticipated consequences. When people stop lusting for one another, the cycle of life is in danger of ending. Fortunately, a speck of the *yeytser hore*'s ashes accidentally blows into the eye of the Chelm melamed, the local elementary teacher, just as he is returning to civilization from seven long years of hibernation that he had undertaken to rid himself of the evil impulse. Cured at last, he is about to take up his angelic existence on earth when this flying ember of lust reinfects him. The narrator, a Hasidic Jew, tells the story in the name of his grandfather, who used to say that "if it weren't for the melamed of Chelm we would have disappeared from the face of the earth long ago."[9]

The erotic principle was thus for Peretz a necessary evil, and not, as it became for Lawrence, a liberating good. However humorously he treated the repressive element in his religious background, he could no more rid himself of his inheritance than the melamed of Chelm could free himself of desire. Standing at the threshold of modern psychology, Peretz knew that at a decisive moment he had subordinated his personal longings—what Freud defined as the libidinous id—to the unvoiced demands of his mother, who also represented his highest model of the selfless Jew. But since his desire for knowledge, carnal and otherwise, had never been extinguished, the conflict continued to smolder, and the pain of renunciation remained ever fresh.

Complicating the emotional attachment to his mother was the special danger to which Jewish civilization was exposed. To some extent, the threat of dissolution was common to all traditional or semitraditional societies at the end of the nineteenth century, and every son who rebelled against his parents was upending not only the family but its way of life. Yet for Jews the threat was compounded. Subject to the same processes of urbanization, industrialization, and secularization that were revolutionizing all European peoples, they were held responsible by many Europeans for the distress of modernity itself. Economically rooted as they were in the towns and cities, politically marginal to and religiously suspect by the Christians, the Jews seemed to profit most by modern reforms, and could thus be blamed for having fostered them. In such an atmosphere, the filial Jew had to assume responsibility not only for his beloved mother but for a despised mother folk with its despised mother tongue. He could try to universalize this impulse, claiming to be the protector of all the oppressed rather than of his particular people. But if he was an honest son, he would have to admit the failure of this strategy, because at the vanguard of Jew hatred were usually the oppressed themselves, resisting the Jew as strenuously as he tried to embrace them.

Peretz was not eager to confront anti-Semitism. As a spokesman for educational reform and social advancement, he was forever urging his fellow Jews toward greater contact with gentile civilization. Along with most socialist sympathizers he preached that the revolt against authority in religion and government would usher in a more tolerant age, that those who had suffered in common would feel a particular kinship in the fraternal society that would emerge. In 1896 he assured his readers that having survived the ancient Egyptian and Babylonian exiles and the bloody massacres of the Middle Ages, the Jews were in no mortal danger *now*. Mankind had progressed from cannibalism to imperialism, which declares war only to market its products.

The old hell with its demons *is* gone, after all, once and for all! We won't be devoured any more, and we won't be enslaved, burned and roasted, chased away. Today the powerful are also human beings; human beings are growing kindlier, wars are growing weaker, and its weapons more human; the life of the weakest is somehow becoming easier and less bitter. . . .[10]

To this liberal credo Peretz adhered, yet he was no fool and no dreamer. Reading the turn-of-the-century Polish press, he saw that such liberal hopes as he had shared with gentile progressive intellectuals were giving way to meaner national instincts and political calculations. The same popular anti-Semitism that installed Karl Lueger as mayor of Vienna and victimized Captain Dreyfus in Paris was all too prominent among Russians and Poles, sworn enemies who had at least this much in common with one another. Both the Polish intellectuals and the peasants had begun to express open antagonism toward the Jews, and scapegoating was likely to be even more important in populist politics than it had been under

79

autocratic rule. Although obviously reluctant to acknowledge these forces of hatred, Peretz had no choice
but to admit them into his consciousness, and into his
writing.

About the time he was writing *Impressions of a Journey,*
a work notable for the absence of any non-Jews, Peretz
had written a sketch of conversations between "himself" the writer and two characters who successively
share his compartment in a mailcoach.[11] The first is an
ignorant and insensitive Jew. The second, a Pole, is a
dear childhood friend whom, in the much-altered cli-
mate of their country, he suspects of anti-Semitism. Although this particular Pole proves himself free of the
taint, he concurs that "Anti-Semitism is being attended
by Politics, a foolish and malicious physician who wants
to prolong her illness." The narrator is poised between
two irritants that are also his formative influences: the
Jewish tradition crying out for improvement and the
Polish reality crying out against the Jew. Significantly,
the subject that links the two conversations is the fate of
the Jewish woman, who stands to be victimized by both
these antithetical forces.

Peretz offered a much more complex view of the problem in a 1903 story called "Stories." Its protagonist is a
Jewish writer, a young man who, unlike Peretz, had
defied his mother's tears in making the break from
home, and is so estranged from his Jewish origins by the
time we meet him that he doesn't realize it is the eve of
Passover until the cashier of the restaurant he frequents
makes a sour comment about "their holiday." While all
around him the Jews of Warsaw rush about in last-
minute preparations, he is preoccupied with a Polish
seamstress he had met in the park some months earlier, a
poor *goye* who lives alone with her hateful widowed

mother and works long days at the machine. Illiterate, and more than a little anti-Semitic, the seamstress tolerates the Jew's company because of the stories he tells her—fairy tales with a happy ending that offer her momentary escape from the troubles of her life. Although she finds him unattractive ("You mustn't dare to touch me. I'm not interested in you. You are so ugly. If you touch me I'll scream and run away"), she allows herself to be entertained by him because he is so adept at spinning romantic illusions.

In anticipation of the visit the seamstress is to pay him that evening, the writer is plotting in his mind a complicated fairy tale about the search of a prince for a sleeping princess on a mountain. This fable—in some ways reminiscent of the symbolic stories of Nahman of Bratzlav, about the many distractions that keep a man from his true purpose—suggests a nation's unsuccessful struggle for liberation, or an artist's vain attempt to capture a perfect work. The intrusion of Passover on the Jew's consciousness, however, provokes a stab of homesickness and turns his mind away from mistress to mother. During his first years in Warsaw, driven half insane with loneliness, he had gone home for the holiday to attempt a reconciliation with his parents, only to be repelled once again by the chauvinism of the Passover story. At dawn on the third day of the holiday he had fled without saying good-bye to his father. His tearful mother turned up at the station to see him off.

Since then two years had elapsed. Now, climbing the stairs to his room, he is assaulted by a vision of his mother blessing the candles and weeping over him. Instead of the story he has been composing all day for the seamstress, he begins to spin a version of one of the many blood libel legends in which the Jews stave off a

Christian plot to destroy them: Festive Jews around a Passover table are startled by a sudden pounding on the door. Instantly alert to the danger, the patriarch locates the corpse of the Christian child that had been planted there by pogromists, and orders his family and guests to cut up and devour the evidence. When the police are forced to leave empty-handed, the assembled guests raise their voices in the *Shfoykh khamoskho*—Pour out Thy wrath on the nations that do not know You—the very prayer of national aggressiveness that had driven the young Jewish writer initially from his parents' home. He is frightened by his own imagination; and convinced that his pen is "too weak" for such a statement, he tries a second, softened version of the blood libel story, substituting miracle for militancy. (At the point that the child is discovered under the table, the Baal Shem Tov, who in this version has come to the seder as an unbidden guest, commands the murdered child to rise, to don a robe and skullcap, and to sit down among them and read. When the pogromists break down the door, once again there is nothing to find.) In these imaginings the Jewish son, who had been responsible for destroying his parents' Passover, projects his own destructive urges onto the even more destructive anti-Semites, and then invents patterns of rescue to save them from harm.

And so, when the seamstress finally knocks at the door asking whether he has any stories, he answers that he has "all kinds."[12] Trapped in the kind of masochistic love that Somerset Maugham described in *Of Human Bondage,* and the actor Emil Jannings immortalized in *The Blue Angel,* Peretz's protagonist never completes either the Polish romance or the Jewish tales. His unresolved conflict between sexual attraction to a Polish

woman and love for the abandoned Jewish mother results in artistic impotence. He punishes himself for having abandoned his mother, his only guaranteed source of
love, by loving a woman who rejects him. The prejudice of the seamstress, which appeals to him because he,
too, longs to free himself of the Jewish burden, also
invites him to collude in the destruction of his people.
Peretz, who knew this conflict from the inside, presents
it here from the outside, in a critical study of the man
who will never satisfy either side of his divided self.

Peretz was not quite that man. But the dichotomy he
sets up in this story, between fairy tales with happy
endings to enchant despairing women and powerful national folktales to protect threatened Jews, provides a
telling glimpse into his own artistic laboratory. At the
time this story appeared, Peretz had begun to publish his
folkstimlekhe geshikhtn, a series of modern folktales based
on traditional sources that may be said to combine the
impulses of universal enchantment and national protection, or the desire to satisfy the seamstress's need for
escape and the Jewish mother's demands on his loyalty.
These tales were popular with almost all segments of the
population. Even some of the social reformers and political activists were prepared to overlook their supernatural conceits for the boost they gave to national dignity
and to liberal conscience, whichever of the two they
considered more important.

These tales offered fundamental reassurance about the
moral order of the universe. Once upon a time, in
Turbin, there was a pious *treger,* or porter, who could
barely feed his family.[13] One miserable Thursday, facing
a Sabbath without a morsel of food in the house, he is
accosted by a stranger with a strange proposal: the porter is to be granted seven years of plenty, but he must

decide *when* they should be delivered. Does he want them immediately, while he is strong enough to work, or later, when he is old and weak?

The good porter says he cannot choose without first consulting his wife. The wife is the principle of economic reality in Yiddish fiction, and Haskalah literature had poked merciless fun at uxorious husbands. Here however, the appeal of husband to wife is made in the name of domestic harmony, and each member of the family reaches a decision according to what is best for the others. Because their children have been sent home from cheder for want of tuition, the wife asks for the money here and now. So the porter goes to the market to report his wife's decision, and by the time he returns home, his children have discovered golden coins in the sand.

In these modern folktales by Peretz, the supernatural event is only background for human miracles that are manifest on earth. When the stranger returns seven years later to tell the family that their years of plenty are over, the wife greets him with perfect equanimity: "We never even began to enjoy our good years because we never treated the gold as ours. Only what a person earns with his ten fingers is really his, and unearned treasures are no more than a trust fund for the poor." Apart from offering charity, she took money only to pay for her children's study of God's Torah, which He may be expected to subsidize. Now let God hand over His treasure to a trustier guardian. But when the prophet Elijah (for of course he is the stranger of all these tales) consults with heaven, much as the porter did with his wife, it is agreed that the treasure should stay right where it is. The moral order of the universe is thus confirmed not in heaven but on earth, where Jews are by now so imbued with the spirit of God's Torah that if He will but grant them bare subsistence, they are capable of maintaining His civilization on their own.

Many of the stories offer similar reassurance that the liberal ethic has taken over from the Divine imperative. When the angels of good and evil come to accompany a couple of dying Jews to their proper places in heaven and hell, it turns out like this: the religious hypocrite who stole from the poor is exposed and taken to hell, but the man who did lifelong acts of charity (cheating just a little on Jewish custom) *chooses* to go to hell to help the sinners, because in heaven there would be nothing for him to do. [14] In one story after another, Peretz implies that whereas religious injunctions guarantee a standard of justice, secular Jews aspire to an even higher standard of mercy.

Through such manifestations of goodness, the Jews also triumph over their enemies. The wicked Polish nobleman may sport with his subject Jew while his licentious wife tries to lure him into her bed, but Jewish morality invariably triumphs over Christian authority. [15] Sh. Ansky, the former Narodnik revolutionary who said that he had been returned to Jewishness by Peretz's writings, developed an anthropological theory about the Jewish emphasis on spirit. Contrasting the physical hero of European imagination with the exclusively moral hero of Jewish folklore, Ansky suggested that the Jews have an unparalleled yearning for transcendent perfection. [16] Ansky might well have been basing his theories on these neo-folktales by Peretz, which go much further than anything he had previously written in emphasizing the supremacy of spirit over matter, and by implication, of the Jew to those who wielded power over him. Because these tales are set in a legendary past, there is no neces-

sary connection between the malicious Polish landown-
ers of his fiction and the Poles with whom Peretz and
Ansky were coming into contact. Nevertheless, implicit
in Peretz's tales (and explicit in Ansky's commentaries)
is an idea of Jewish moral potency that compensates for
Jewish political impotence.

In the year before he began his *folkstimlekhe geshikhtn,*
Peretz under the pseudonym "The Bee" took over
from the older Yiddish writer Mordecai Spector a
weekly column called "Cities and Towns."[17] Essayistic
reportage was then a popular feature of the Yiddish
press. When Peretz took over from Spector, he continued his predecessor's practice of organizing news and
information from regional informants into a composite
picture of Jewish life in Poland. But the Bee had much
more stinging intent. He exposed Hasidic rabbis and
modern doctors who played on the credulity of those
who truly needed help. He needled the warring Jewish
political factions of every city, town, and village, for
squandering resources that should have been aiding the
poor. Peretz reported on the desperate condition of Jews
in towns that had been bypassed by the railway, on
abandoned foundlings and abused children, and on pogroms, epidemics, local scandals, and national dangers.
At one point, bitter in despair, Peretz said he felt lucky
to be a Jew, since it had accustomed him to looking at
the grim side of life; how could he deal with the news if
he were any less prepared for its horror?[18]
    One column, the eighteenth in the series, describes a
visit from one of his readers, Bobbe Yakhne, the grand-
motherly counterpart of "Grandfather Israel," who
symbolized the older generation of pious Jews. Bobbe
Yakhne complains to the writer that she is as dry as a

spent wet nurse, having had to pawn the last of her jewelry to provide a dowry for her daughter and an army exemption for her son. Instead of helping her in this time of need, the Bee is now adding to her miseries by undermining Jewish pride and spirit. Peretz tries to justify himself, explaining that rabbis are his target because of the importance of a shepherd to the fate of his flock. He, who takes no particular pleasure in flaying the Jews, is only doing his duty by standing guard where he has been placed.[19]

The *folkstimlekhe geshikhtn* were a different kind of response to Bobbe Yakhne's complaint, as though Peretz was trying to restore to granny some of her lost grandeur—if not her pawned earrings and headband then at least the proud spirit in which she once wore them. Abandoning realism altogether, and with it the need to stand guard over his contemporaries, he tries to remind the Jews of their divine mission by rekindling their faith in the essential values of that mission—kindness, charity, humility, honesty, love, and the optimism that faith engenders. In the earlier Hasidic tales he had used as narrators the disciples of spiritual masters, small witnesses to someone else's greatness. These were modeled on the stories that Hasidim tell one another about their rabbis. Here, much like the Hasidic rabbis themselves, Peretz assumes the full-bodied voice of omniscient invention:

There once dwelt in Safed a Jew of great wealth and good fortune, who traded in jewels, diamonds, and other precious stones. He was truly a man of great wealth, not like the upstarts of our day.

This Jew lived in a palace of his own, with windows that shone like gleaming eyes upon the Sea of Galilee; and about this palace bloomed a magnificent garden with all manner of beautiful trees and fruits. Songbirds sang in the sky, and on the earth there grew aromatic herbs that were a joy to behold and of much use in healing. Wide paths, strewn with golden sand, wound through the garden, and over these paths the crowns of the trees wove into one another to form a canopy of shade. Little arbors in which one could rest lay scattered along the edges of the garden, and in the ponds, which glistened like mirrors, there swam the rarest and whitest of swans. It was an earthly paradise.[20]

The most striking feature of Peretz's garden of Eden story is his leisurely narrative style, as if the impatient author had deliberately adopted a Sabbath pace to set this fiction apart from all his workaday prose. So, too, every other element of the narrative is festive and opulent. Reb Chiya, the owner and inhabitant of this earthly paradise, is not rich in the manner of modern parvenus, but ideally endowed with wisdom, learning, and goodness, as well as material possessions. The Jewish world encompassed by this story is no dingy historical shtetl or threatened European community but a "time and place that never was" when great yeshivas flourished simultaneously in Jerusalem, Safed, and Babylon, and Jewish merchants traveled freely across all the deserts and seas. Like all Peretz's fiction, this adult fairy tale turns on moral choices and moral disclosures, but within a context of nobility, endless space, and eternity.

"Mesiras nefesh," the title of this story, means self-sacrifice, devotion unto death, fathomless love. Although Peretz had often treated love before, the love motif of this story was on a much higher plane, with three romances interwoven into the tale of a sinner who must win redemption. Given certain thematic and

Hope and Fear

structural similarities between them, Wagner's *Tann-häuser*—a performance of which Peretz saw in War-saw—might have been the inspiration for this contrast-ing Jewish version.[21]

Chananya is the perfect Jewish scholar. But shielded from responsibility by his mother's uncritical love and goaded to arrogance by an unscrupulous teacher, he uses his cleverness to confound the Torah rather than as a tool in its service. For this crime he must pay heavily: he is stripped of all his knowledge and condemned to exile in the desert. Only after a lengthy penance, and thanks to the intervention of Elijah, is he permitted to take up the study of the aleph-bet again. He comes to the ye-shiva of Reb Chiya as the humblest and most ignorant of students to relearn everything he has forgotten, labori-ously this time, in selfless devotion to Torah.

More tenacious and devoted than Chananya is his bride Miriam, Reb Chiya's only daughter, who chooses this humble beggar over all the other scholars because she is attracted by his purity and his pain. She marries him despite having discovered that heaven intends to take him away from her a week after their marriage, as final payment for his sin: he is to be redeemed only posthumously through the child that will be born to her. One day in the garden—that same luscious garden to which we were introduced at the start of the story—Miriam overhears the snake making its plans to poison her husband. Dressed in her husband's clothes, she sets out to fool the viper, and endures its poisonous bite undetected. Her death causes great consternation in heaven, which tolerates no such "mistakes" and orders her immediately back to life where she belongs. Mir-iam, however, does not intend her sacrifice to have been in vain. Not until she extracts from heaven the promise that Chananya will be spared does she agree to return to earth, and to undergo at the end of her life the death throes that will again await her.

Fairy tales are replete with final reversals where evil is punished and goodness rewarded. In these fairy tales, as we have seen, the true miracles are wrought not by the supernatural powers but by human beings, who challenge heaven's justice with a putatively higher standard of mercy. Miriam's devotion, which forces heaven to bend its laws, becomes the validation and source of Torah itself. The story thus inverts the biblical text where Eve, fallen prey to the snake's temptation, invites Adam to share in her sin. Miriam's selfless love redeems the false intelligence that uses learning as an instrument of power, and false sexuality that uses lust to corrupt. Miriam the wife is just such a hallowed Jewish mother as Peretz describes in his memoirs, and in placing her at the heroic center of his Jewish myth he is ascribing to her the ultimate value from which all others flow. Intellectual prowess, the male domain, depends for its moral confidence on the female's self-sacrificing love. This is what Peretz established as the hierarchy of Jewish values.

It is easy to be lulled by the *folkstimlekh* quality of these tales into a mood of national self-congratulation or quasi-religious solace. As "tales in the folk manner" they have a comforting style, and their narrative scheme allows for homiletic interpretation, though only as part of a richly complicating dialectical process. The reader who is sensitive, for example, to the Kabbalistic images in "Mesiras nefesh," will be reading a psychological study about the nature of human values within a web of mystical questions about the possibility of redemption. Much as the political point of the story of "Bontshe shvayg" was blunted by the aura of sanctity that still clung to the main character, the morally rational scheme of this story of Eden is clouded by a secret language of transcendent quest. All the time that Jewish life was becoming increasingly polarized and politicized, Peretz was tunneling out a new art from sources mysterious as well as programmatic. The critics, through a scheme of periodization, tried to distinguish the engaged social activist of the 1890s from the neo-romantic of the 1900s, the Hebraist from the Yiddishist, the reliable secularist from the recidivist orthodox Jew, ignoring the modern temper that remained in perpetual quarrel with itself.

Perhaps the most characteristic Peretz invention is the soul that can be permanently admitted neither to heaven, because it has not done enough good, nor to hell, because it has not done enough evil, and is therefore condemned to drift unconsigned between this world and the next. This soul has been formed by a religious consciousness that still longs to believe in the knowable difference between good and evil, and still yearns to be admitted into the heaven of such a moral universe; but being a truly modern soul, it can no longer trust in the heaven it aspires to enter. This wandering soul provides a rather different view of devotion, of healing *mesiras nefesh,* in a story that stands as bitter counterpoint to the triumphalism of Miriam's self-sacrifice.

The unconsigned soul of "The Three Gifts" pleads with heaven's gatekeeper for some alternative—any alternative—to the fate of perpetual exile.[22] Thus it is advised to return to earth and seek out three perfect gifts for the saints, who being no longer as incorruptible as saints once were, are happily susceptible to bribes. As it turns out, these gifts are almost impossible to find, because if heaven is no longer what it was, human life on earth was never much to begin with, and the soul spends what seems like half an eternity looking for the appropriate presentations. Then, one by one, he finds them: a Jew with a knife at his throat is killed when robbers mistake his refusal to yield his treasured bit of Eretz Yisroel earth for what they believe must be priceless jewels; a Jewish woman, condemned by Christians for violating their streets with her presence, asks to have her skirts pinned to her flesh, so that when she is dragged by horses to her death she should not be violated by Christian eyes; and a Jew made to run the gauntlet goes back to retrieve his skullcap rather than reach freedom bareheaded, and thereby proves the superiority of his faith to the power of the whip. In each of these episodes a Jew sacrifices himself with genuine *mesiras nefesh* for the different aspects of Jewish nationhood, morality, and faith; and the three bloodied gifts of a grain of earth, a needle, and a skullcap, duly proffered, gain for the errant soul its entrance into heaven. Here, as in other tales, Peretz highlights the contrast between the decaying religious superstructure and the earthly Jews who manifest truly moral instincts in spite of it. It is possible to read this story as evidence that Jewish moral values will triumph over Christian might. But do the three blood-soaked gifts really promote an ideology of martyrdom, or do they decry an ideology of martyrdom? If the borrowed self-sacrifice of fellow Jews is all that can gain the modern soul its final resting place, then perhaps it would be better advised not to apply to heaven's gate at all. Doubt in the form of the soul has been loosed in the world, and the saints hardly put it to rest when they accept its "beautiful but impractical" sacrifices. The story does not put it to rest either.

Hope and Fear

His friends tell us that Peretz often applied to himself the parable of a princess who, whenever she reaches out to stroke an animal in her garden, or to smell a flower, or to pluck a fruit from the tree, finds it turned to ashes in her hand.[23] This romantic image is striking for the way it yokes exceptional endowment to exceptional deprivation. Refinement and sensitivity, which open the door to all that is most exquisite in life, may also keep one from enjoying its pleasures, since they also prevent one from tasting simple satisfaction.

Although Peretz seemed larger than life to those around him, he did not find his life large enough. He wanted to be both the truest son of his people and a conqueror of new worlds. He was torn between law and literature, between the engaged, political enterprise of a public figure and the need to retire into the mystery of himself. As a writer he was both the leading Jewish publicist of his day and the first genuine modernist, refusing to accept public communication as the sole criterion of art, and looking to the subconscious for truths that eluded him in realistic narrative. He loved Hebrew, which linked him to the regal beginnings of the Jewish people. He was wedded to Yiddish in the same gritty spirit that he was loyal to his job and his wife. He always longed to be accepted into Polish in cross-cultural amity. This last goal proved the most elusive, depending as it did on forces utterly beyond his control.

The many contradictory elements in his nature that made it so difficult for his contemporaries to pin him down also prevented the author from finding one genre, one style, one set of themes through which best to express himself. There did not appear to be enough pseudonyms to contain all the voices he wanted to assume: the progressive Dr. Shtitser who champions modern science; the Bee that spares no one its sting; Orphan of Nemirov, appealing to compassion and charity; Editorial Mischief who tries to achieve a bantering tone; and, at the other extreme, Israel Shvermut, the Jew of heavy heart. Peretz also presented himself as Lucifer, and in a host of other disguises. [24]

His restlessness intensified during the final decade of his life. Those who knew him well and those who met him for the first time remarked on unpredictable aspects of his behavior and sudden turns of mind. Some observers ascribed his changeability to growing older, with its accompanying resentment of the younger writers whom he had helped to promote. Certainly, the more famous he became and the more precious he felt his time to be, the more he chafed at the imposed restrictions of the bureaucratic job which limited his visits to other communities and sapped his creative energies.

Always prepared to explore the warring facets of his personality, even to the point of questioning his sanity, Peretz knew that the social problems he undertook to address in his writing also contributed to his unease. "Hope and Fear" was the title of his seminal address to Jewish socialists in 1906: "My heart is with you," he applauded the revolutionary determination of the younger generation. [25] Here was a movement that had transformed his inchoate social criticism and religious reformism into a firm ideological program, and now stood poised to enact a political revolution. But as we have already pointed out, precisely this was at the heart of his fear. Mankind was not an army that could be subdued through ideological conquest. If the socialists were ever victorious, they in turn would stifle human freedom, and become tyrants in the name of egalitarianism: "Terrifying

Hope and Fear

will be your defense of the equal rights of the herd to the grass beneath their feet and the salt above their heads, while you will target as your enemies: free individuals, supermen, creative geniuses, prophets, liberators, poets and artists. . . ." Peretz was the first political thinker within the Jewish milieu to recognize that the struggle for emancipation under the tsar was being taken over by forces that would continue to stifle rather than promote individual liberty; that idealism was not a sufficient standard for ideas. Nietzsche's promotion of the human will against the forces of reductionism (echoes of which can be heard in this essay) must have encouraged Peretz in his own call for heroic spirit.

Peretz's participation in the Conference on the Status of Yiddish, held in Czernowitz the last week of August 1908, brought to a head another set of hopes and fears. The invitation that he received from the international organizing committee in New York had filled him with dismay.[26] Much as he wanted Yiddish to become the national language of the Jews, he felt that it still lacked some of the requirements to substantiate that title. He objected to the exaggerated claims the organizers were making for Yiddish, and to their practical agenda. The difficulties that still faced the Yiddish language if it was to become the Jewish lingua franca required that a working conference consider such substantive issues as standardized spelling, an official grammar, a proper dictionary, and the needs of the Yiddish press and theater. Peretz felt that Yiddish could never serve as the national language of the Jews unless the Tanakh, the complete Hebrew Bible, were available in excellent Yiddish translation. As part of that effort he had set himself the task of translating the five megillot—Esther, Ruth, the Song of Songs, Ecclesiastes, Lamentations. He wanted such immediate projects as a Yiddish Bible translation to be accorded prominence on the conference agenda instead of vague resolutions and inspirational generalities.

Despite his doubts, Peretz dominated the conference. In his keynote address he offered his most optimistic assessment of the Jewish future within the larger European context. The legitimation of Yiddish meant, in the first place, that the Jewish masses were coming into their own: the unlearned Jew was liberating himself from the domination of the Jewish scholar and man of wealth, completing the revolution that the Hasidic movement had begun in the eighteenth century; the Jewish woman was freeing herself from subjugation to male authority; the Jewish worker was learning his self-worth, and consolidating his strength. The process of democratization and political self-transformation that other nations had undertaken was now consolidating among the Jews through the instruments of their culture.

As for this Yiddish-speaking Jewish people, its hopes lay in the decline of the state and the corresponding rise of the nation, the folk. Multilingual Czernowitz was the ideal venue for a Yiddish conference, because as one of the great cities of the multinational Austro-Hungarian Empire it was a harbinger of things to come: "The 'folk,' not the state, is the modern byword. . . . The nation, not the fatherland! Its unique culture rather than its patrolled borders guarantees a nation its independent existence."[27]

But Peretz could not control the conference, much less the political development of Europe. Delegate attention centered not on practical initiatives, as he would have wished, but on the wording of what came to be the main resolution. When the acrimonious debate came to a head, Peretz used his prestige to ensure that Yiddish was declared *a* national language of the Jewish people rather than *the* national language, as the delegates of the Socialist Bund insisted. Nevertheless, almost all reports of the conference lingered on the ideological conflict that had destroyed what was to have been a manifestation of solidarity. That Yiddish, which he had always regarded as the instrument of national cohesion, should now become one of the chief weapons of internal Jewish conflict caused Peretz great distress. Having invested his hopes for the Jewish national future in the development of a unique national culture, Peretz feared an internal Kulturkampf that would explode all its prospects. His tempered embrace of Yiddish, like his modified embrace of Socialism, once again earned him the suspicion of the younger ideologues. Hebraists accused him of betraying the Jewish national future while Yiddishists accused him of chauvinism, conservatism, and religious backsliding.[28]

At the same time that young radicals began to use Peretz as a target representative of the reactionary past, a powerful voice of Jewish orthodoxy also singled Peretz out for trivializing the sacred. By the time Hillel Zeitlin moved from Vilna to Warsaw in 1908, he was already a major force in Polish Jewish journalism as the standard-bearer of modern orthodoxy; his arrival meant that there were now two literary "homes" in the city where Peretz had formerly held solitary court. Having experienced very much the same crisis of faith as Peretz and other modern Jewish intellectuals, followed by the obligatory period of self-education in modern philosophy, social science, and literature, Zeitlin had resolved at least part of the conflict with modernity by remaining an observant, practicing Jew. The "Letters to Jewish Youth" that he began publishing, first in the Warsaw *Haynt* and then from its founding in 1910 in the Yiddish daily *Moment,* appealed to the same youthful audience that Peretz was trying to reach, but through a more philosophically coherent program of religious peoplehood. "Peretz has a heaven," Zeitlin wrote, "but in his heaven there is no God." The accuracy of this barb can be gauged not only by the speed with which it circulated (for that might have had baser motives) but by the heat of Peretz's counterattack.

Peretz made Zeitlin's accusation the cornerstone of one of his most famous polemical essays, "Paths That Lead Away from Jewishness," published in the Warsaw Yiddish daily *Der fraynd* between March and May 1911. While joining forces with Zeitlin in citing assimilation as the greatest modern peril facing the Jews, he accuses orthodoxy of being the first of the paths that diverts the Jew from his Jewishness by turning what was once a living force into a stockade.

> What do you want, Khumesh-with-Rashi preacher, to bring back yesterday? Stifler of change, do you want to extend today beyond its borders and lock tomorrow out? Do you know what this can be compared to? Take the living seed whose shell has cracked, and instead of replanting it in order to make it blossom more beautifully, cram it back into its shell, bind and wire it shut, and chant an incantation: "Grow, you seed, in confinement and darkness."[29]

Peretz tries to turn Zeitlin's accusation into a weapon against him by equating Jewish religion with the artificial dead shell and his own cultural "Yiddishkayt" as the living earth in which the seed will flourish. According to to Peretz, it was the Christian Church that arrested creative Jewish development when it locked Jews away in the ghetto and prevented them from having "contact with life." Those who try to save the *shul,* the traditional synagogue, are thus the ironic servants of the Church: they are preserving the caricature that Judaism became under pressure of the Church, because they lack confidence in the Jews' adaptive resilience.

Read today, Peretz's essay "Paths That Lead Away from Jewishness" is less the guide to the perplexed that he intended than a monument to his own intellectual and artistic anxiety. The anxiety is everywhere in evidence. Although he sets out in apocalyptic terms to describe a pressing social problem, he presents us with no evidence of its severity, no idea of its scope, nor any definition of its nature. One-sentence paragraphs reveal how ill prepared the author is to explain any of his thoughts in detail, or to build a consistent argument. No attempt is made to summarize or confront the positions of his antagonists—Zeitlin included—who had attacked Peretz for what he avowedly *was;* and Zeitlin is attacked by Peretz as a "khumesh-with-Rashi" reactionary, which he demonstrably *was not.* Peretz argues through an explosion of images, metaphors, homilies, and quips, with a passion that does not obscure an underlying confusion of ideas. The unresolved tension that sometimes mars and other times enhances Peretz's fiction makes him an unreliable cartographer of the "paths" he sets out to chart.

As for Zeitlin's accusation, Peretz dons it with pride. Heretics and blasphemers can become "greater than the gods" when they carry inside them the divine spark and use it to become partners in Creation. He was certain that transposed into culture, the values of a religious civilization could continue to serve the purposes of "heaven," with artists as the modern prophets, speaking in the name of the God within themselves. Peretz dazzles in his attacks on stagnant Judaism. But nowhere does he confront the political or social or even cultural implications of the Jewish humanism he was advocating within a political context of intensifying antagonism. The appeal to God on the part of traditional Jews was rooted in their belief that God's power was supreme, and that He would ultimately if not immediately redress the balance of power in their favor. Implicit in the Jews' faith was trust in the might of the Almighty God. Peretz consigned the Jews to a heaven as weak as they were.

All this was despite the fact that by the time he wrote this essay, Peretz's anxieties derived most of all from his Polish compatriots and the tsarist regime to which they were alike subject. On this front Peretz had always waged his most complicated campaigns, against total assimilation on the one hand, for integration into Poland on the other. His idea of the modern folk or the modern nation was theoretically ideal for the Polish context in which it had evolved, since the Jews and Poles had shared the same soil for hundreds of years, and during the national uprising of 1863 had even demonstrated their common opposition to the same repressive regime. If each people could now continue to draw from its distinct religious heritage and forge a modern national identity in its own language, together they could realize their creative autonomy side by side. Peretz never faltered in his struggle on behalf of the Jews, and saved his most scathing polemics for Jews who traded in their identity through religious or cultural conversion. Much less noted by Peretz scholars and biographers was his equally fierce loyalty to mother Poland, and his resistance to any geographic or political alternative to local coexistence.

Hope and Fear

Here Peretz was to suffer his most crippling disappointment. Although a parallel modern Polish nationalism was indeed emerging, it sought political autonomy and homogeneous national institutions. Peretz might be satisfied with the cultural distinctiveness of peoples living side by side, but the majority of Polish nationalists of both the populist and the rightist parties wanted an independent Polish state with patrolled borders and a forceful army and all the machinery of political statehood. What is more, they resented the Jewish presence in Poland at least as much as the unwanted tsarist regime. Once the Church began to lose its power to modern political parties, opposition to Jewish influence became an almost irresistible part of Polish self-definition as Polishness was transposed into ethnic terms. Unable as yet to win their freedom from the Russians, many Poles began to speak out forcefully against the Jews for corrupting their nation from within.[30]

Anti-Semitism became an overt issue in the election to the Duma of 1912, which is now recognized as the watershed in the development of Polish attitudes toward the Jews.

[The election] raised ethnic tensions substantially in Warsaw and in the whole Kingdom and led to an extensive economic and social boycott of Jews by Poles. It marked the increasing politicization of the "Jewish question," and strengthened the place of antisemitism in the Polish nationalist movement. It spelled the end of acceptance by important parts of the Polish nationalist movement in the Kingdom that the Jewish assimilationists were effective and worthy allies.[31]

When the socialist Jagiello was elected over the nationalist Kucharzewski, many Poles blamed the Jews for having deprived them of a representative who would have advanced the Polish cause in the Russian Duma. Their anger boiled over in an economic boycott of the Jews backed by a forceful anti-Semitic campaign.

Peretz followed these political events very closely.[32] He considered the tsar's introduction of parliamentary procedures—however imperfect—at least a step in the right direction, not least because it allowed Jews to participate in the political process. During the preelection campaign, Peretz had argued that a coalition of progressive Jews and Poles could build up a strong basis for the democratic, autonomous Poland of the future. The leaders of the Warsaw Jewish community, those whom Peretz attacked as assimilationists, had urged a boycott of the election on the grounds that Jewish involvement in so charged an atmosphere would bring disaster to the community. Although Peretz used his first postelection analyses to attack his familiar Jewish antagonists, the boycott and the backlash soon forced him to confront the truth of their prediction. "We are always dependent on the non-Jewish will," he conceded.[33] Professed Polish nationalists had made anti-Semitism the main plank of their election platform, and even Polish liberals who had once expressed tolerance for the Jews in their midst now adopted anti-Semitic slogans in projecting their own views of the Polonized future. Peretz's optimistic prophecy at the Czernowitz Conference that enfranchised national minorities in a multinational Europe would replace the declining national state had proved utterly mistaken in his own city.

Peretz began to look his past hopes squarely in the face. Aleksander Świętochowski had been one of the leading voices of Warsaw positivism in the 1880s, when as the exponent of tolerance he had invited all Poles, including the Jews, to work together. That tolerance, Peretz now realized, had been predicated on the idea that Jews would assimilate into the Polish majority. "But Świętochowski is also a clever man who studied . . . at the University of Leipzig and therefore knows that a certain amount of water can tolerate only a certain amount of salt; when there is too much salt, a residue remains unabsorbed, and the Polish nation will not be able to absorb the whole Jewish mass. . . ." The hostility of the Polish press forced Peretz to recognize that even progressive Poles now considered the Jews superfluous. And while he still thrashed about for a way of *satisfying* these liberal objections to the Jews, he was rejected at every turn. He writes of Świętochowski:

> Now there is no way at all of accommodating him, because should you suddenly recall that you once had a home where you might have been salt without salinating the foreign waters, and should you propose to move back there, the same Świętochowski leaps up in a blaze of anger: "He will not allow his country to be treated as a guest house for the night. Poland is not a hostel."
>
> So you say: Dear Świętochowski, if you like, we shall stay, but because we are much salt and you so little water, we will remain unabsorbed. . . .
>
> He lets out a roar like a lion: *shtsures! [szczurowaty]* (rodents!). . . . So we become rodents.
>
> And that's not the worst of it. His students come and say: "It's true that you have the right to a distinctive life of your own. Every nation has that right. But we Poles will have to expel you from our land . . . or fight to destroy you. . . ."[34]

There seemed to be no way out; the Jews could no more satisfy Polish nationalism by leaving for Palestine than by staying in Poland. The Poles declared themselves as betrayed by the one as they were frightened by the other. Peretz concluded his political articles on a note of determination, urging the Jews to resist the temptation of assimilation. "Blood is not water!" he cried, rejecting the image of the dissolving salt, and reaffirming Jewish national dignity. To those Jewish readers who were made nervous by his attacks on Polish anti-Semites he gave the high sign of mockery: "This Yiddishkayt with a shrunken heart, whose cremated liberal hopes and Messianic aspirations rest under the ashes without a single remaining Jewish spark, with no trace left of the *pintele yid* except for a drop of fear—mute fear—this Yiddishkayt wants us to be quiet! These Jews ask us for pity's sake to keep silent. We do have pity—on them! As for us, we must triumph."[35] Anti-Semitism strengthened Peretz's national resolve. If accepted as allies, the Jews would join the Poles, he said, now as in the past. But as long as the Poles pressed for their dissolution, the Jews would stiffen their Jewishness.

In "Paths That Lead Away from Jewishness" he offered the following parable: once upon a time, in ancient Greece, the city of Sparta was under siege. Realizing that they could no longer hold out against the enemy, the community elders sent to Athens for reinforcements. Instead of the expected troops and weapons, Athens sent only a single man—the hunchback Pindar. But this single man was enough to turn the tide of battle. Standing in the public square, Pindar the poet sang such a hymn to battle that he fired young and old with the courage and patriotic love to defeat the enemy.[36] Peretz-Pindar determined to do the same for his besieged people. As the modern folk evolved from the ancient religious community, culture would have to take over from religion, and poets from preachers and rabbis, in ensuring Jewish survival.

In this atmosphere of impending catastrophe Peretz worked on his poetic drama, *Bay nakht oyfn altn mark* (*Night in the Old Market Place*), which some modern readers consider to be the greatest of his works.[37] It is a phantasmagoric vision, a "fevered dream" of despair, in which all the facets of Peretz's creative spirit, and all the major characters of his imagination, are animated to dramatize the nightmare of Polish Jewry. Following his travels through the Jewish towns in 1890, Peretz had experimented several times with the artistic image of "death-in-life," pushing the metaphor as far as it could go toward literal description of the economic, political, and cultural wasteland he had discovered. Now he had the dead emerging from their graves to mingle onstage with the living, in a reversal of Ezekiel's famous prophesy that the dead bones would some day come to renewed life. As in all great tragic drama, the force of creative imagination is directed ultimately toward the redemption of the doom that is being portrayed. But it is hard to escape the grimness of its vision.

Peretz also wrote his memoirs at this time, recalling the home where he had once felt himself too confined, and where he now located the source of such solace as there could be. In this bleak spirit, he translated the Book of Lamentations.

Peretz had begun his career as a Yiddish writer with the story of Monish, a boy who yields to the temptation of gentile music and ends nailed to the stake in hell. He returned to that theme in one of his last short stories, "Yom Kippur in Hell," about a Jewish cantor of Lahadam, the town that never was, who is blessed with an extraordinary voice. Otherwise undistinguished, the cantor "has only to ascend the prayer stand and lift his voice in prayer and behold, the entire congregation is made one mass of wholehearted repentance. . . ." Much as Satan feared that the moral perfection of Monish would make him superfluous in a messianic age, so Satan resents the cantor for inspiring sinners to repentance before they can be snatched to hell. Resorting to black magic, he robs the cantor of his voice.[38]

Although he is no match for the devil, the cantor is so angered by this cosmic injustice that he determines to have his revenge. He commits suicide, but at the point of dying when he regains his splendid voice long enough to say his confession, he deliberately refrains from using it on his own behalf in order to ensure his admission to hell. There, on Satan's ground, and with his voice restored, he intones the final confession so persuasively that all the condemned souls melt into goodness and win their posthumous release. Not that the narrator of the story believes the devil can be permanently outwitted. Hell, he assures us, was soon repopulated by a new generation of evildoers. But a tiny temporary victory is scored.

Peretz's cantor does not deserve his evil fate any more than he deserved the marvelous gift of his voice (or any more than modern Jews deserve to be the target of political demons on earth). Until he is pricked by Satan's malice, the cantor doesn't give the slightest thought to the moral purpose he serves. Only when injustice strikes him personally does he become engaged in the struggle of good and evil, sacrificing himself with a kind of heroism that far exceeds his ordinary capacities. In the rage of this Jewish cantor, Peretz with his own fine voice allows us to feel the final snap of Jewish patience when injustice becomes intolerable.

Hope and Fear

We see how desperately Peretz, expecting nothing more from God, tried to find some spiritual recourse for the Jews within the human sphere. God's impotence is on full display here: the soul's struggle on Yom Kippur, the holiest day of the year, is not subject to either divine judgment or mercy. At "Neila," the final service of Yom Kippur when the gates of heaven presumably close on God's verdict, the cantor acts unassisted to turn the tables on Satan. Peretz had once entertained similar fantasies about the mission of the Jews: "Perhaps we are the messiah-people who will be liberated right at the end, along with the lumpen-prole?" In this story, set at the eleventh hour of history, the Jew experiences only a flashing victory in the darkness of hell.

Peretz tried to fashion a modern Jewish culture rich enough to compensate for the decline of religious tradition, the absence of political power, and the steadily rising waves of social ostracism, violence, hatred. He turned his energies to the founding of Jewish institutions—choirs and music societies, theater companies and dramatic groups, open universities and literary circles—that involved ordinary Jews in the creation of culture rather than providing culture for them. Finally, even such cultural projects had to give way to plain efforts of rescue. When new streams of refugees flooded Warsaw at the outbreak of World War I, driven from the border towns by the occupying armies and by tsarist accusations of their disloyalty, Peretz worked himself to a frenzy improvising soup kitchens and supervising the orphanage he had helped to establish. On his desk when he died were lines of an unfinished children's poem, one of over a hundred that he had already composed.[39]

With no political alternative to offer the Jews, neither

the hope of an independent land in Palestine nor eventual assimilation into a classless society, Peretz tried to strengthen Jewish spirituality by interpreting even hardship as a force of potential good. One of his last poems was a *dudele,* a parody of the intimate song that the great Hasidic leader Rabbi Levi Yitzkhok of Berdichev had addressed to God. Peretz's *dudele* assures God that although the rabbi-shepherds had not been able to keep the Jewish flock from jumping the fences, these bad times—by which Peretz means these anti-Semitic times—are certain to keep the flock penned in. Beneath the irony of this prayer of solace is a terrifying unintentional irony, for Peretz really tried to believe that the Jews could be morally strengthened through political adversity.

Peretz died on April 3, during the intermediate days of Passover 1915. The estimated hundred thousand Jews who accompanied his funeral cortege to the cemetery represented every ideological and organizational faction, a posthumous tribute to the inclusive idea of the modern Jewish people he had tried to promote. Long after his death he remained the emblem of a Jewish cultural polity. Schools, orphanages, and publishing houses in all parts of the world were named for him. Many more books and articles were published about him than about any other Yiddish writer. The anniversary of his death was everywhere observed by memorial services, and in Warsaw by a massive annual pilgrimage to his grave.

His characters became part of modern Jewish discourse. Monish, Bontshe, the Rabbi of Brisk and the Rebbe of Biale, Shloyme and Leah of *Di goldene keyt,* the Chelemer teacher, the Mad Talmudist, the Wanderer, the Suicidal Housewife, the Pious Cat, Leib Konskivoler the religious hypocrite, Mendel Braynes the pious exploiter of his wife's labor, and a host of others became

Hope and Fear

as real to modern Yiddish and Hebrew readers as Oliver
Twist and Mr. Pickwick were to modern English readers, as David and Jonathan had been to the ancestors of
both English and Jews. His work and his example inspired some Jews to hope that cultural politics was a
viable means of national survival.

On the twenty-fifth anniversary of Peretz's death,
Grininke beymelekh, the Yiddish school publication of
Vilna, put out a special volume of I. L. Peretz for youth.
It opened with Peretz's parable about Pindar's rescue of
Sparta that the editors had excerpted from the newspaper article in which it originally appeared and published
under the title "Der zinger—der ziger" ("The Singer,
The Victor").[40] With this story of the poet who had
roused a nation to victorious self-defense, the educators
of Vilna hoped to evoke the analogous image of Peretz
and to inspire in their students a similarly effective resistance. The year was 1940, briefly after the Russians had
turned the city over to the Lithuanians and before it was
conquered by the Nazis.

There was a problem with Peretz's parable that neither he nor his admirers recognized but that we who
follow are obliged to note. The Sparta of his homily had
a polity and an armed force to which Pindar could appeal. Culture in that situation was only a supplement,
not a substitute, for national power. While Peretz was
shaping an earthly culture that outrivaled heaven's in its
goodness, others were shaping an earthly culture that
outrivaled hell's in its venom. The schoolchildren of
Vilna and of all Poland were murdered with the words
of Peretz on their lips.

Notes

Wherever possible, I have followed the spelling of the *Encyclopedia Judaica*. Terms and names appearing in Yiddish or Hebrew are transcribed according to the system of the YIVO Institute for Jewish Research in their Ashkenazic pronunciation. Thus Isaac Leib Peretz becomes Yitskhok Leybush Perets when his Hebrew and Yiddish works are cited.

Since *The I. L. Peretz Reader* (ed. Ruth R. Wisse; New York: Schocken, 1990) was still in production when this manuscript was submitted, I could not cite page numbers when referring to its contents. Unless otherwise indicated, the Yiddish writings of I. L. Peretz are cited according to the Kletskin edition of his Works, *Ale Verk* (Vilna, 1925–29), 18 vols.; the Hebrew writings according to the Dvir edition of his Works, *Kitvey y. l. perets* (Tel Aviv, 1926–27). The standard sources of Yiddish literary biobibliography are Zalmen Reyzn, ed., *Lexikon fun der yidisher literatur, prese, un filologye* (Vilna, 1926–29), 4 vols.; Shmuel Niger and Jacob Shatsky, eds., *Lexikon fun der nayer yidisher literatur* (New York: CYCO, 1956–81), 8 vols. Hereafter: Reyzn *Lexicon* and CYCO *Lexicon*.

Introduction

1. N(achman) Meisel, "Perets mit unz" ("Peretz with Us"), in *Tsum tsveytn yortsayt fun y. l. perets* (Kiev: Nissan, 1917), p. 8.

2. Yoysef Volf, *Leynendik peretsn* (*Reading Peretz*) (Buenos Aires: Central Organization of Polish Jews in Argentina, 1948), p. 99.

3. Melekh Ravitch (Bergner), *Dos mayse bukh fun mayn lebn* (*The Storybook of My Life*) (Tel Aviv: Perets farlag, 1975), p. 10.

Reason and Faith

1. Letter from Peretz to his cousin Moyshe Altberg, tentatively dated by the editor 1887–88. In Y. L. Perets, *Briv un redes (Letters and Speeches)*, ed. Nachman Meisel (New York: YKUF, 1944), p. 129. Hereafter: *Briv un redes*.

2. Yeshaye Margulis, untitled memoir in *Perets bukh* (Vilna, 1940), p. 308. Reyzn *Lexicon*, 2:992, lists accusations, one or more of which may have led to his disbarment: Peretz was neglecting his law practice; he was denounced by local orthodox Jews who could not forgive his "apostasy"; a Polish competitor denounced him on charges of Polonization (i.e., of encouraging the use of Polish over Russian).

3. On Peretz's cultivation of a Polish appearance see Ben Avigdor (A. L. Shalkovitch), *Miseyfer zikhronotay (From My Memoirs)*, *Hatsefira*, 1919. On a recent trip to Zamość, I was struck by Peretz's resemblance to the bust of Count Zamoyski in the courtyard of what was once the Zamoyski family residence.

4. This information is conveyed in Peretz's letters to Sholem Aleichem. See particularly *Briv un redes*, p. 141.

5. *Yidishes folksblat*, 1889, nos. 25–26, p. 23. Cited by A. Gurshteyn, "Peretses ershte trit" ("Peretz's First Steps"), *Di royte velt* 7 (April 1925): 39. The correspondence between Sholem Aleichem and Jacob Dineson shows their pained reaction to Levi's insulting attitude: for example, Dineson to Sholem Aleichem 5/17/88; 5/24/88. Archive LD, Beyt Sholem Aleichem.

6. Peretz said that he heard of Sholem Aleichem's publication from his friend Epstein, who was, according to I. D. Berkowitz, an employee at the printing shop in Berdichev where *Di yidishe bibliotek* was being published. *Briv un redes*, p. 138.

7. N(aftali) Vaynig, "Poylishe lider fun y. l. perets in yor 1874" ("I. L. Peretz's Polish Poems of 1874"), *Perets bukh*, pp. 191 ff. In a letter of December 3, 1911, to the historian I. Tsinberg (who was collecting material for the Russian Jewish Encyclopedia), Peretz wrote: "[I] started out writing Polish (published nothing, burned what I wrote)—it was an internationalist moment—threw it aside, it was alien, took up He-

Notes

brew which felt lifeless, passed over to Yiddish." *Briv un redes,*
p. 321.

8. [Gavriel Yehuda Lichtenfeld and Y. L. Perets], *Sipurim beshir veshirim shonim* (*Poetic Tales and Miscellaneous Poems*) (Warsaw, 1877).

9. *Briv un redes,* p. 155.

10. Ibid., p. 141.

11. See David G. Roskies, "An Annotated Bibliography of Ayzik-Meyer Dik," in *The Field of Yiddish,* 4th collection, ed. Marvin I. Herzog et al. (Philadelphia: ISHI, 1980), pp. 117–234. Sholem Aleichem's attack on Yiddish potboilers is in *Shomers mishpet* (*Shomer's Trial*) (Berdichev, 1888).

12. The attitudes of Yiddish writers to their language are described by Dan Miron, *A Traveler Disguised: The Rise of Modern Yiddish Fiction in the Nineteenth Century* (New York: Schocken, 1973).

13. Magda Opalski and Israel Bartal, *Dialogue of the Deaf* (working title), describe shifting images of Poles and Jews in one another's literatures in relation to the uprising of 1863. I am grateful to the authors for letting me read this work in manuscript.

14. Piotr S. Wandycz, *The Lands of Partitioned Poland, 1795–1918* (Seattle: University of Washington Press, 1984), pp. 260–72.

15. *Briv un redes,* undated letter, p. 139.

16. Ibid., p. 149.

17. Y. L. Perets, "Monish," in *Di yidishe folksbibliotek,* ed. Sholem Aleichem (Kiev, 1888). For a discussion of the variants of this poem see Chava Turniansky, "Di gilgulim from y. l. peretses 'monish,' " *Di goldene keyt,* 1965, no. 52, pp. 205–24. Trans. (based on variant of 1908) by Seymour Levitan, in *The Penguin Book of Modern Yiddish Verse,* ed. Irving Howe, Ruth R. Wisse, and Khone Shmeruk (New York: Viking, 1987), pp. 52–81.

Gurshteyn, "Peretses ershte trit," p. 31–34, describes the negative reception of the poem on the part of Simon Dubnow and Sholem Aleichem.

18. Y. L. Perets, *Mayne zikhroynes,* p. 7.

19. Ibid., pp. 126–34.

20. Y. L. Perets, "Der meshugener batlen," in *Bekante bilder*

(*Familiar Pictures*) (Vilna, 1903). Trans. "The Mad Talmudist" by Irving Howe and Eliezer Greenberg, eds., *A Treasury of Yiddish Stories* (New York: Viking, 1954), pp. 231–42.

21. Jacob Shatzky, *Geshikhte fun yidn in varshe* (*The History of the Jews in Warsaw*) (New York: YIVO, 1953), 3:80–88.

22. Nahum Sokolow, "Yosl hameshuga" ("Mad Yosl"), *Hatekufa* 26 (1930): 61.

23. Y. L. Perets, *Bilder fun a provints rayze in tomashover paviat in yor 1890*, in *Di yidishe bibliotek* (1892), 2:73–141. In Hebrew, *Kitvey perets*, pp. 117–38. Trans. Milton Himmelfarb, *Impressions of a Journey through the Tomaszów Region*, in *The I. L. Peretz Reader*.

24. Jacob Shatzky, "Tracing the Materials of Jan Bloch's Statistical Expedition" (in Yiddish), *YIVO Bleter* 34 (1950): 296–98.

25. Margulis (untitled memoir, p. 311), writes that in Tomaszów-Lubelsk they did their work even though a police officer forbade them to gather information. Sokolow, "Yosl hameshuga," p. 61, also notes that they had to get permission from the local constabulary. Israel Bartal describes Peretz's scant and stereotypic use of gentile characters in "Non-Jews and Gentile Society in East-European Hebrew and Yiddish Literature, 1856–1914," Ph.D. dissertation, The Hebrew University in Jerusalem, 1980, pp. 187–204.

26. *Bilder fun a provints rayze*, in *Verk*, 7:9. There are differences in tone between the Yiddish and Hebrew versions. Reb Borukh in Hebrew more closely resembles the religious hypocrite of Haskalah literature who uses prayer to camouflage greed. See, for example, the closing lines of the Hebrew, missing in Yiddish: "Do we do anything at all? Why, of course we do, we study and we pray. . . ."

27. Isaac Bashevis Singer writes that in his childhood it was common to see young men and women reading Peretz with a dictionary: "Often the son would ask his father for an explanation of this or the other expression. The father considered Peretz a heretic, but he was pleased that the son had to appeal to him for the explanation of a talmudic saying." Yitzkhak Varshavski (Singer), "A naye oysgabe fun peretses verk" ("A New Edition of Peretz's Works"), in *Forverts*, July 5, 1947, p. 2.

Notes

28. Letter to Helena Ringelheym, undated (1877), *Briv un redes*, pp. 38–41.

29. *Bilder fun a provints rayze*, in *Verk*, 7:73.

30. Margulis (untitled memoir, p. 311); the reference is to the town of Yartsev (Jaryczów Nowy).

31. Nachman Meisel, *Y. l. perets: zayn lebn un shafn* (*Peretz: His Life and Works*) (New York: YKUF, 1945), pp. 119–34. Meisel claims his examination of the council records shows Peretz began his employment January 1, 1891, at an annual salary of 500 rubles. As a lawyer, his annual income had been as much as 3,000 rubles.

32. For example, in *Di yidishe bibliotek*, vol. 1 (1891): "Gedalye," by Eliza Orzeszkowa, pp. 101–36; "Der yidisher kvestar" ("The Jewish Alms Collector: A Lively Portrait of Vilna"), adapted by Peretz, according to accompanying note, from *Kwestarz Zydowski, Postac Zyjaca w Wilnie*, by Wincent Korotynski, pp. 260–62. In vol. 2 (1891–92): "Chava Rubin," by Władysława Okonski. In vol. 3 (1895): "Mendl Danziger," by Maria Konopnicka, pp. 4–36; "Der dorfsshnayder" ("The Village Tailor"), by L. Klemens Junosza, pp. 51–73. See also Peretz's contacts with Polish ethnographers during the 1890s, Jacob Shatzky, "Perets shtudyes," *YIVO Bleter* 28, no. 1 (Autumn 1946): 40–80.

33. Letter (undated) from Peretz to Dineson: "I would forget that I was the editor of *Folksbibliotek* were it not for the Polish translators who are always asking for permission to translate and to publish [from its contents]." *Briv un redes*, p. 181.

34. Y. L. Perets, "Bildung," opening editorial on education, *Di yidishe bibliotek* 1 (1891): 5–20. Peretz writes that while the enemies of the Jews regarded them as bloodsuckers and revolutionaries, and Jewish chauvinists made inflated claims about the national genius, "we say simply: we Jews are people like all other people! We have certain good qualities and bad. We are neither gods nor demons, but human beings." He said that it was therefore necessary for the Jews to reexamine themselves from this humanist perspective and set out their goals as a modern people.

35. Feuilleton signed "lets fun der redaktsye" ("Editorial Mischief"), *Di yidishe bibliotek* 1 (1891): 227.

36. David Frishman (under pseud. A. Goldberg) emerged as the archcritic of Peretz, with a pamphlet called *Lokshn* (*Noodles*) (Warsaw: Shulberg, 1894), an obvious parody of Peretz's *Yontev bletlekh*. Saul Bellow, though he included three Peretz stories in his anthology *Great Jewish Short Stories* (New York: Dell, 1963), wrote: "I do not wholly admire the stories of I. L. Peretz. This is heresy, I know, but I find them slow going; they depend too much on a kind of Talmudic sophistication which the modern reader, and I along with him, knows very little of" (p. 12).

37. Y. L. Perets, "Mekubolim," in *Der tones* (*The Fast*) (Warsaw, 1894), pp. 3–13. Trans. Shlomo Katz, "Cabalists," in *A Treasury of Yiddish Stories*. The Yiddish version considerably reduces the tendentiousness of the Hebrew original, which appeared in 1891. Gershon Shaked argues for the artistic advantages of Peretz's Yiddish over Hebrew variants in *Hasifrut haivrit 1880–1970* (*Hebrew Narrative Fiction*) (Tel Aviv: Kibbutz Hemeukhad and Keter, 1977), pp. 133–40.

38. Y. L. Perets, "Mishnas khasidim," in *Der yid* May 8, 1902, 11–14. Appeared in Hebrew in 1894. Trans. David Auerbach, "The Missing Melody," in *The I. L. Peretz Reader*.

Nation and Class

1. H. D. Nomberg, *A literarisher dor* (*A Literary Generation*) (Warsaw: Lewin-Epstein, no date), p. 4.

2. Y. L. Perets, *Haugav: shirey ahava* (*The Harp: Love Poems*) (Warsaw: Schwartzberg, 1894). *Kitvey perets,* pp. 495–96.

3. Joseph Klausner, *Darkhi likrat hatekhiya vehageulah* (*My Path Toward Renaissance and Redemption*) (Tel Aviv: Mossad Tel Aviv, 1946), p. 61. Shakhne Epstein, *Dos arbetsfolk in y. l. peretses verk* (*The Working People in the Works of Peretz*) (Ekaterinoslav: Di velt, 1918), p. 12.

4. Nachman Meisel, *Yitskhok leybush perets un zayn dor shrayber* (*Peretz and His Generation of Writers*) (New York, 1951), gives an overall description of relations between Peretz and various individuals and literary groups. The most extensive Yiddish bibliographical archive contained 9,449 items on

Notes

Peretz compared with 5,719 on Sholem Aleichem, 3,401 on Mendele Mocher Sforim, and 6,706 on Abraham Cahan, long-time editor of the *Forverts*. Ephim H. Jeshurin, *Hundert yor moderne yidishe literatur (Bibliography of 100 Years of Modern Yiddish Literature)* (New York: Educational Committee of Workmen's Circle, 1965), p. 605.

5. David Pinski, "Dray yor mit y. l. perets" ("Three Years with Peretz"), *Di goldene keyt* 10 (1951): 22–23.

6. Sholem Asch, "Mayn ershte bakantshaft mit perets" ("My First Acquaintance with Peretz"), *Di tsukunft*, 1915, no. 5, pp. 458–63; see also A. Litvak (Chaim Jacob Helfand), "Di zhargonishe komitetn" ("The Yiddish Committees"), in *Roytn pinkas*, vol. 1 (Kiev, 1920), pp. 109–32.

7. Y. L. Perets, "Nes khanuke" ("The Miracle of Chanukah"), in *Dos likhtl* (Warsaw, 1895), pp. 17–28. *Verk*, 2:90–97.

8. Y. L. Perets, "Mendl braynes," in *Di yidishe bibliotek* 2 (1892): 26–34. "Kas fun a yidene" ("A Woman's Rage"), in *Di yidishe bibliotek* 3 (1894): 35–41.

9. Y. L. Perets, "Dos Shtrayml" ("The Rabbinic Fur Hat"), in *Literatur un lebn*, 1894, pp. 119–34.

10. Y. L. Perets, "Di frume kats" ("The Pious Cat"), *Verk*, 6:21–24. "A farshterter shabes" ("A Destroyed Sabbath"), *Der varshever yidisher kalendar*, 1893, pp. 71–77. *Verk*, 2:16–24.

11. Ben tamar (Peretz), "Kritik," in Abraham Reisen, ed., *Dos tsvantsikste yorhundert (The 20th Century)* (Warsaw, 1900), p. 94.

12. Y. L. Perets, "Bontshe shvayg," in *Literatur un lebn*, 1894, pp. 11–22. Trans. Hillel Halkin, "Bontshe Shvayg," in *The I. L. Peretz Reader.*

13. Ezra Mendelsohn, *Class Struggle in the Pale* (Cambridge and New York: Cambridge University Press, 1970), p. 49. Shmuel Niger, *Yitzkhok leybush perets*, pp. 232–46, describes the impact of Peretz's writing on the workers' circles.

14. When the story of Bontshe was dramatized in the Broadway production, *The World of Sholem Aleichem* [*sic*], a halo of light was cast on him as he made his request. (The producers evidently felt that a work by Peretz could be included in the "world" of Sholem Aleichem with no violence to either Yiddish author.)

15. Y. L. Perets, "Di arbeter lage in London" ("Report on Working Conditions in London"), *Dos likhtl* (Warsaw, 1895), p. 3.

16. Meisel, *Y. l. perets: zayn lebn un shafn*, pp. 167–68. Meisel's biographical account should, however, be used with caution.

17. Mordecai Spector, *Mit y. l. perets in festung* (*With Peretz in Prison*) (Odessa: Farlag literatur, 1919).

18. Ibid. Spector, who made light of the imprisonment, accused Peretz at the time of playing the martyr: "Since Peretz spent time in prison he's become quite mad. Before, as you know, he was already well on his way, but since his imprisonment he wants to play the martyr, though he was no more guilty than you or I. . . ." Letter to Ravnitski, Hebrew University National Archive, 401185, dated Warsaw, May 1, 1900.

19. Pinski, "Dray yor mit y. l. perets," pp. 5–31, gives a vivid account of the years 1891–94.

20. *Briv un redes*, p. 212.

21. Report of Purim ball in *Der yid*, March 22, 1900, pp. 7–8.

22. Y. L. Perets, "Hofnung un shrek" ("Hope and Fear"), *Der veg*, May 18, 1906. *Verk*, 8:226–29.

23. Shatzky, "Perets shtudyes," pp. 46–65.

24. Shmuel Niger (Charney), *Yitzkhok leybush perets* (Buenos Aires: Argentine Branch of the World Jewish Congress, 1952), p. 274.

25. Y. L. Perets, "Tsvishn tsvey berg," subtitled "Between the Rabbi of Brisk and the Rebbe of Biale; a Simchat-Torah story told by an old teacher," *Der yid*, October 4, 1900, nos. 40–41. Trans. Goldie Morgentaler, "Between Two Mountains," in *The I. L. Peretz Reader*. It is worth noting that in his column "Shtet un Shtetlakh" for August 28, 1902, also in *Der yid*, Peretz attacks the current Rebbe of Biale for having bowed to pressure from another Hasidic leader in revising his earlier ruling that his ritual slaughterer was unfit because his hands trembled. The column is one of many chronicling contemporary Hasidic abuses and stupidities.

26. Nomberg distinguished between Peretz's earlier spontaneous Hasidic stories and these later ones that he found forced.

Notes

A literarisher dor, p. 14; *Y. L. Perets* (Buenos Aires: Central Organization of Polish Jews in Argentina, 1946), p. 108. Gershon Shaked defines these tales as didactic fiction, *Hasifrut haivrit,* pp. 153–55.

27. Spector, *Mit y. l. perets in festung,* p. 61, recalls that Peretz expressed envy for him and the writer M. I. Berdichevsky because their fathers were Hasidim, and they knew the movement from the inside. He felt the lack of this firsthand knowledge in himself.

28. The fuller treatment of Peretz's relation to Zionism that Nahum Oyslender called for in 1925 ("Peretses shtet un shtetlakh," *Tsaytshrift,* Minsk, vol. 1, p. 65) is still wanting. Although Peretz considered the colonization projects in Palestine a hopeful prospect, he could not see mass emigration as a solution for the Jews as a whole.

29. Peretz actively resumed writing Hebrew in 1903, apparently under influence of Joseph Klausner, who came to Warsaw to assume editorship of the periodical *Hashiloakh.* He contributed to *Hatsofe,* 1903–5, took active part in the celebration of Nahum Sokolow's jubilee in 1904, and negotiated for publication of his Hebrew writings. In a letter to Sholem Aleichem, dated Warsaw, January 14, 1904, Bialik says Peretz told him that from then on he intended to write his better things in Hebrew. *Iggerot khayim nakhman bialik (Letters,* ed. P. Lakhover) (Tel Aviv: Dvir, 1938), p. 203.

30. Peretz was one of three judges along with Klausner and A. L. Levinsky. *Hatsofe: Kovets Sipurim (The Spectator: Prizewinning Stories)* (Warsaw, Markheshvan 29, 1904).

31. Peretz translated Bialik's poem under the title "Masah Nemirov" ("The Oracle of Nemirov") for the Yiddish newspaper *Der veg,* to which he was then a contributor. He apologized to Bialik for the "mistake" in the translation, explaining that he had asked a young writer of his acquaintance to provide a rough translation of the poem because he was short of time, never thinking to check on his trot. Letter dated January 31, 1906, *Briv un redes,* pp. 222–23. Sholem Aleichem's comment, "No one could have ruined a work to this extent unless he had intended to do so," is cited by his son-in-law Isaac Dov Berkowitz, in *Dos sholem aleichem bukh (The Sholem Aleichem Book)* (2d ed., New York: YKUF, 1958), p. 175.

Klausner describes Peretz's reworked version of the poem and the reaction it provoked in *Darkhi likrat hatekhiya vehageulah*, p. 116.

32. Y. L. Perets, "Khurbm beys tsadik," *Hashiloakh* 11 (1903): 471–74, 566–70; 12 (1904): 529–43. Letter of Bialik to Ben Zion Gutman, January 21, 1904, *Iggerot Bialik*, p. 206.

33. Y. L. Perets, *Di goldene keyt* (The Golden Chain: A Drama of Hasidic Life in Three Acts), in *Di velt* (Vilna), 1907, no. 2, pp. 1–71. In *Verk*, 3:95–188. See Peretz's dramatic writings and the history of their performance in Zalman Zilbertsvayg, *Lexikon fun yidishn teater*, vol. 3 (New York: Farlag Elisheva, 1959), pp. 1898–2076; for the history of *Di goldene keyt* and its forerunner, *Der nisoyen* (*The Temptation*), see pp. 1910–41.

34. A. Litvak (Helfand), "Y. l. perets: pesimizm un tragisher optimizm," in *Literatur un kamf* (*Literature and Battle*) (New York: Veker, 1933), pp. 112 ff.

35. B. Gorin, "Y. l. perets a matone lekoved zayn 60tn geburtstog" ("A Present for I. L. Peretz on his 60th Birthday"), *Zukunft*, 1911, pp. 393–94.

36. David Bergelson, "Briv tsu der yunger yidisher inteligents" ("Letter to the Young Jewish Intelligentsia"), in *Di yidishe velt*, April–May 1915, p. 43.

37. Y. L. Perets, "Hisgayles oder di mayse fun tsignbok" ("The Story of the Billygoat"), *Verk*, 5:185–92. Trans. Maurice Samuel in *The I. L. Peretz Reader*.

38. Michael Steinlauf, "Jews and Polish Theater in Nineteenth Century Warsaw," *Polish Review* 32, no. 4 (1987): 439–58. I have also had the benefit of reading unpublished chapters of Steinlauf's work on the Yiddish theater of Warsaw.

Hope and Fear

1. Y. L. Perets, *Mayne zikhroynes*, in *Verk*, 12:6. The following information about Peretz's childhood is based on this source.

2. Dovid-Hirsh Roskies, "A shlisl tsu peretses zikhroynes" ("A Key to Peretz's Memoirs"), *Di goldene keyt* 99 (1979): 132–

Notes

59, provides a critical study of the memoir as a "masterpiece of artistic modernism."

3. *Mayne zikhroynes*, p. 133.

4. Jacob Glatstein, "Peretses yerushe" ("Peretz's Legacy"), in *In toykh genumen* (*Sum and Substance*) (New York: Farband, 1947), pp. 493–94.

5. Y. L. Perets, "Vos hert zikh?" ("What's New?"), in *Di yidishe bibliotek* 2 (1891): 5–10, describes the pervasive anti-Semitism in Prussia and Austria (and by implication in the tsarist empire), but although he says that colonization is a matter of life and death for the Jews, he expresses extreme caution about every prospect of emigration.

In an undated letter (1892?) to Jacob Dineson, who was living without a residence permit in Kiev, Peretz writes that he should look into the possibility of emigration to Argentina, and would certainly do so were a position offered, but in the meantime he found it easier to work for others than on his own behalf. *Briv un redes*, pp. 182–83. There are many expressions of Peretz's interest in visiting Palestine from about 1903. See, for example, the postcard to his childhood friend, Dr. Isaac Gelibter, dated Warsaw, July 10, 1911, thanking him for the suggestion of a four to five week trip to Palestine, but saying that the proposed time was inconvenient and too brief. *Briv un redes*, p. 293.

6. Di Bin (Peretz), "Shtet un shtetlakh," *Der yid*, August 21, 1902, p. 11.

7. *Briv un redes*, p. 84.

8. Y. L. Perets, "Venus un shulamis," *Di yidishe folks-bibliotek* 2 (1889): 142–47. *Verk*, 4:89–95. Trans. Seth Wolitz, in *The I. L. Peretz Reader*.

9. Y. L. Perets, "Der chelemer melamed," *Di yidishe folksbibliotek* 2 (1889): 126–29. *Verk*, 2:6–9.

10. Dr. Shtitser (Y. L. Peretz), "Undzer treyst un hofnung" ("Our Comfort and Hope"), in *Di treyst* (*Comfort*) (Warsaw, 1895–96), p. 30. *Verk*, 17:175–76.

11. Y. L. Perets, "Inm post-vogn," *Di yidishe bibliotek* 1 (1891): 21–40. *Verk*, 4:96. Trans. Golda Werman, "In the Mail Coach," in *The I. L. Peretz Reader*.

12. Y. L. Perets, "Mayses," *Der fraynd*, 1903, no. 131, p. 2.

Verk, 2:159–74. Trans. Maurice Samuel, "Stories," in *The I. L. Peretz Reader*. The Hebrew version is strikingly different. When the seamstress asks whether he has any stories, he says that he has two—one horrible, the second not quite as bad. She asks, "And have you no princess?" He replies, "She was here, but she is gone, vanished" (*Kitvey peretz*, p. 257). This suggests that the Jew has given up the attempt of winning the seamstress.

13. Y. L. Perets, "Zibm gute yor" ("Seven Good Years"), *Der fraynd*, 1904, no. 91, p. 2. *Verk*, 1:37–42.

14. Y. L. Perets, "Baym goyses tsukopns" ("At the Bedside of a Dying Man"), *Der fraynd*, 1904, no. 237, pp. 2–3. *Verk*, 1:5–12.

15. Israel Bartal shows that these historical stereotypes are used by Peretz as a foil for Jewish values, to dramatize the conflict between "Jew" and "Gentile" ("Non-Jews and Gentile Society," pp. 147–67).

16. Sh. Ansky (Rapoport), "Der yidisher folks-gayst un zayn shafn" (based on a lecture given in Vilna, November 8, 1918), *Gezamlte shriftn* (*Collected Works*) (Warsaw: Central, 1925), 15:15–28.

17. Peretz took over from Spector, who wrote under the pseudonym *emes* (truth), in the issue of May 8, 1902.

18. Y. L. Perets, "Shtet un shtetlakh," *Der yid*, August 14, 1902, p. 14.

19. Perets, "Shtet un shtetlakh," *Der yid*, September 18, 1902, p. 9. Nahum Oyslender thinks that Bobbe Yakhne represents the corruption of Jewish values. Her jewels are "false" because she has long since traded them in for inferior glass. "Peretses 'Shtet un shtetlakh,' " *Tsaytshrift* (Minsk, 1925), p. 70. The text does not really bear out this interpretation, stressing as it does the poverty of the woman and the losses that she has incurred through no fault of her own.

20. Y. L. Perets, "Mesiras nefesh," *Der fraynd*, 1904, nos. 273, 275, 279, 281, and 286; pp. 2–3 throughout. *Verk*, 1:155–90. Trans. "Devotion Without End," by Irving Howe and Eliezer Greenberg, eds., *A Treasury of Yiddish Stories*, pp. 118–48.

21. Nahum Sokolow describes having attended a perfor-

Notes

mance of *Tannhäuser* in Warsaw where he met Peretz. *Perzenlekhkeytn* (*Personalities*) (Buenos Aires, 1948), p. 171.

Sol Liptzin calls this story "a Yiddish version of the Tannhäuser theme and the Alcestis theme in a most original combination," and analyzes their similarities. *Peretz* (New York: YIVO, 1947), pp. 23–29.

22. Y. L. Perets, *Di dray matones*, in *Verk*, 1:13–24. Trans. Hillel Halkin, "The Three Gifts," in *The I. L. Peretz Reader*.

23. Nomberg, *Y. l. perets*, p. 37.

24. A list of Peretz's Yiddish and Hebrew pseudonyms can be found in Saul Chajes, *Thesaurus Pseudonymorum Quae in Litteratura Hebraica et Judaeo-Germanica Invenientur* (Hildesheim: Georg Olms, Verlag, 1967).

25. Perets, "Hofnung un shrek," *Verk*, 8:226–29.

26. *Di ershte yidishe shprakh-konferents* (*The First Conference on the Yiddish Language: Reports and Documents of the Czernowitz Conference of 1908*) (Vilna: YIVO, 1931), pp. 4–5.

27. Ibid., p. 75.

28. Ibid. contains reports of immediate responses to the conference and Peretz's role. A detailed study of reactions to Peretz would provide a useful guide to shifting ideological patterns in 1905–25.

29. Y. L. Perets, "Vegn vos firn op fun yidishkayt" ("Paths That Lead Away from Jewishness"), *Verk*, 17:89. This passage is translated by Michael C. Steinlauf.

30. For a partial bibliography of the growing attempt to assess Polish anti-Semitism, see George J. Lerski and Halina T. Lerski, eds., *Jewish-Polish Coexistence, 1772–1939: A Topical Bibliography* (Westport, Conn.: Greenwood, 1986), pp. 128–36.

31. Stephen David Corrsin, "Political and Social Change in Warsaw from the January 1863 Insurrection to the First World War: Polish Politics and the 'Jewish Question,' " Ph.D. dissertation, University of Michigan, 1981, pp. 274–75.

32. Peretz's weekly column "In mayn vinkele" ("In My Corner"), in the Warsaw newspaper *Haynt*, beginning May 17, 1912, and extending into the following year, was devoted in large part to the elections of October 15, 1912, for the fourth Duma and the turmoil that followed.

33. Y. L. Perets, "In mayn vinkele," *Haynt*, May 28, 1912.

34. Ibid.

35. Perets, "In mayn vinkele," *Haynt*, June 7, 1912.

36. Y. L. Perets, "Vegn vos firn op fun yidishkayt," *Verk*, 11:77.

37. Y. L. Perets, *Bay nakht oyfn altn mark* (*Night in the Old Market Place*). The definitive edition and interpretation of the play is Khone Shmeruk's *Peretses yiyesh vizye* (*Peretz's Vision of Despair*) (New York: YIVO, 1971). This work is one of the few reliable editions of Peretz and an invaluable source for the study of all Peretz's writings.

38. Y. L. Perets, "Ne'ilah in gehenem," *Di yidishe velt*, January 1915. *Verk*, 15:166–72. Trans. Hillel Halkin, "Yom Kippur in Hell," in *The I. L. Peretz Reader*.

39. Y. L. Perets, *Verk*, vol. 13 (*Lider un baladn*), contains about 100 children's songs and rhymes written during the last months of the author's life.

40. *Y. l. perets far kinder* (*Peretz for Children: on the 25th Anniversary of the Author's Death*) (Vilna: Grininke beymelekh, 1940).

Index

PARENTHESES INDICATE a pseudonym (following a personal name) or the author's name (following a title). Titles without the author's name in brackets are of works by Peretz himself.

Index

Rapoport. *See* Ansky, Sh.
Reisin, Abraham, 39
Ringelheym, Helena. *See* Peretz, Helena
Roman Catholicism, 98–99, 101

Sefer Habris (Hurwitz), 46
Shaikevitch, N. (Shomer), 7
Sholem Aleichem (Rabinovitch), 61, 74; criticism of Peretz, 29; founds *De yidishe folksbibliotek*, 5–8; humorous writing, 28–29; liberalism, 8; Peretz's correspondence with, 7, 10–11
Shapiro, Lamed, 39
Shomer (N. Shaikevitch), 7
Shtitser, Dr. (Peretz pseudonym), 93–94
"Shtrayml, The" (The Rabbinic Fur Hat), 45
Shvermut, Israel (Peretz pseudonym), 94
Socialism, 51–55, 94–95
Sokolow, Nahum, 18–19, 26
Spectator, The (newspaper), 60
Spector, Mordecai, 74, 86; arrest and imprisonment, 52, 53
"Stories," 80–83
Sutzkever, Abraham, xv
Świętochowski, Aleksander, 4–5, 102–3

Tannhäuser (Wagner), 89
Theater, 68–69
"Three Gifts, The," 91–92
Travels of Benjamin III, The (Abramovitch), 4
Trunk, Yekhiel Yeshaye, 39
"Tsvishn tsvey berg" (Between Two Mountains), 58

Uniates, 3

"Venus and Shulamith," 75–77
Vilna Ghetto, xv, xvi

Wagner, Richard, 89
Warsaw Ghetto: Peretz's influence in, xvi
Warsaw Jewish Community Council, 26, 69
Warsaw pogrom (1881), 10, 18
Weissenberg, Itche Meir, 39
What Is To Be Done? (Gavrilovich), 45
Wincheski, Morris, 52
"Woman's Rage, A," 44
Women's issues, 44–45
Wulf, Joseph, xvi

Yehoash. *See* Bloomgarten, Solomon
yid, Der (weekly), 57
Yiddish: conference on, 95–97; influence of anti-Semitism on, 8–10; literary resurgence, 5–6; popular press, 5, 41, 57; position in Jewish society, xvii, 8–10, 97; theater, 68–69
yidishe bibliotek, Di (periodical), 27–28, 41–42
yidishe folksbibliotek, Di (periodical), 5–8
Yidishes folksblat (newspaper), 5
"Yom Kippur in Hell," 105–7
Yontev bletlekh (periodical), 41, 42–43, 52, 53

Zeitlin, Hillel, 97–99
"zinger, Der—der ziger" (The Singer, The Victor), 109
Zionism, 59–60, 69
Zionist Conference (1897), 57